# PRODIGAL HUSBAND
by Tom Ashcraft
with Max Call

Gift Publications
Costa Mesa, California 92626

**Prodigal Husband**

Copyright © 1980 by Gift Publications

Published by Gift Publications
Costa Mesa, California 92626

Library of Congress Catalog Card Number 80-67300
ISBN 0-86595-002-4

*Printed in the United States of America*

Bible references are taken from the King James Version.

*This book is dedicated to the glory of God in heartfelt thanks for my wife Elizabeth. She is a priceless gift that He's given to me.*

**Thomas L. Ashcraft**
**Houston, Texas**

# Acknowledgments

*Some names of people mentioned in this book have been changed to protect the privacy of individuals and/or their families.*

# CONTENTS

# FOREWORD

I don't even know the "prodigal husband" in this book.

Then why am I writing a foreword for it?

About halfway through the pages that follow, the man I didn't know died to his old self and was born again. For 25 years, I have known and loved the new Tommy: a Christian gentleman, successful large bakery owner and founder of the world's largest chapter of Full Gospel Business Men's Fellowship International, the Atlanta Chapter.

Today Tommy is a Full Gospel vice president, completely dedicated and devoted to Christ, to his lovely wife Elizabeth and their family. Tommy has put aside his career in business for what he considers a more important career—spreading the Word—offering his Christian testimony, training chapters in leadership and giving courses in rallies and conventions.

The Full Gospel Business Men's Fellowship has grown to its present size on every continent in the world through the dedication and untiring work of men like Tommy Ashcraft.

Many times Tommy and I have traveled to Fellowship conventions in the United States, Africa, Asia and Europe, frequently with our wives. When you travel so much with a man, you get to observe everything about him.

I have never seen a person of more purity than Tommy. He is

*i*

a man of God who loves his wife, family and the whole world. He is so dedicated to Christ that I cannot picture him as the person he says he was in the book. A miracle from Christ was needed to turn him around 180 degrees to make him a new person.

*Prodigal Husband* could not have been published at a better time. Severe pressures and strains are breaking up marriages and destroying homes faster than ever before. Now, in the United States, one out of two marriages ends in divorce.

Tommy shows how and why marriages break up and the best ways to preserve or restore them. Strong families make up strong nations.

This exciting and practical book will be a blessing to the millions, and I heartily recommend it—not only to those with problem marriages. It will also awaken those with good marriages to their blessings and to a new thankfulness to God.

Today Tommy and Elizabeth are effective marriage counselors. God has given Elizabeth and Tommy great wisdom and understanding. They make a fine team.

And even Tommy's life before he was born again is useful. The past has given him many insights helpful in the present—reasons for problem marriages and solutions for them.

Wherever Tommy offers his Christian testimony or teaches—and he is an excellent Bible student—he has amazing appeal, particularly at retreats for men.

Those fortunate enough to hear him love him. He is in constant demand. Now Tommy can be met in a new form—this book, which I feel will also be in constant demand.

Demos Shakarian

Founder/President
Full Gospel Business Men's
Fellowship International

# Chapter 1
# FLIGHT INTO THE PAST

*". . . if sinners entice thee, consent thou not."*
**Proverbs 1:10**

Completing four weeks of daily meetings in four capital cities of Europe, I boarded my British Caledonian Airways evening flight at Heathrow Airport just outside London. For the next 11 hours, the wide-bodied DC-10 would run a losing race with the fading sunset all the way to Houston, Texas. Pretending an interest in the ground activity outside my window, I studied my own reflection in the darkening glass.

My true age wasn't evident in what I saw. I still had a full head of black hair and my brown eyes were still sharp. Fastening my seatbelt, I was aware of my thickening waist, but the lines in my face weren't deep. Most people missed guessing my age by about 10 years. It was my one vanity not to correct their thinking.

The flash of startling white robes over my reflected shoulder distracted my thoughts. A man in Arab garb, minus a burnoose, had taken the seat beside me. There was something familiar about him. His eyes were warm, and in the glass his hair and beard appeared soft and flowing. I felt his smooth hand touch mine on the arm of my seat and turned to speak. The seat was empty!

With my hand still warm from the touch, my eyes filled with silent tears. As always, I wasn't alone. Jesus was flying with me.

In that brief moment, He allowed me to feel the comfort of His companionship. I heard the voice in my heart say, "You've done well, Tom Ashcraft, and I'm pleased." Settling back in my seat, I spoke to the voice in my heart.

"I haven't always done well, Lord."

"Think about that, Tom," the voice said. "Remembering that all things are of Me, have you ever done anything I haven't redeemed?"

With a heart full of love, I turned my thoughts inward and softly murmured, "You're my Lord and I will obey."


I was born at a place called Rose Creek in western Arkansas on April Fool's day. I was the second of six children. My older brother, Ernest, died when he was two and a half leaving me alone with my father and mother for a little over two years until Frank was born. My three sisters, Ann, Alpha and Jo, followed with about four years separating each. We were a poor but happy family. My parents, Cornelia and Byron, provided for us as best they could on an eighty-seven acre farm. Dad added to our meager income by selling dry goods door to door during the winter and butchering the livestock we raised and selling the meat.

We were poor but lacked nothing. My mother provided a tender, enduring love, and my father was there with the stern, loving discipline that's needed by every growing boy. We never went hungry, but our table fare was solid and simple. Two pairs of bib overalls and one pair of new shoes each year was the basis of my wardrobe. Frank was the same and mother made all the girls' clothes as well as her own on her old pedal-driven Singer.

Sitting in the cabin of a DC-10 while it taxis for takeoff is a far cry from the unpainted, four-room house that was my boyhood home. Using a mixture of water and flour for paste, mother had papered all the inside walls with pages from the "Arkansas Gazette." Resting on high rock pilings, the house provided shelter for some of our small livestock during the sudden summer and winter storms. Feeling the thrust of the airplane's jet engines reminded me of the power and roar of some of those storms.

Closing my eyes as we raced down the runway, I let my memory take me back to the summer of my fifth year. The Archduke Francis Ferdinand had just been assassinated in Serbia, but that wasn't nearly so important to me as were the dark clouds boiling in the sky south of our farm in Arkansas. Once again, I could feel my mother's arms around me and experience the power of her prayers. As the cyclonic roar grew in my young ears, we huddled together beside the old iron bed in our living room and she held her hand up to the storm, boldly praying, "God, stay Your hand! God, stay Your hand!"

When the storm passed, we went outside to a scene of total desolation. Everything was gone. The smokehouse just 20 feet away was smashed. The fences and barn were down, but not one shingle, board or window on the house was damaged. Father came running from the field; he'd lain in a dry ditch and escaped the storm. Finding my brother Frank, my mother and me safe, he praised God for His mercy and led us all in the search for our stock.

This experience led me to understand, in my impressionable young mind, that Mother had a direct pipeline to God and that He paid attention to her prayers. When any praying was needed, I knew my mother would take care of it. She became my shelter from all danger. Her Christian faith was all I needed to feel safe. She was worthy of all the love I could give her. I considered God to be like my father, stern and quick to punish. Mother was the one person who possessed the power to soften both God and man. She became the basis of my faith. Whenever danger threatened, I would run to her, leaving my father in the fields with the other hands, giving them an excuse to run also. If it rained or there was a bad storm, I wasn't punished for running, but if I'd caused needless panic, I was firmly told, "Go cut a hickory!"

With Mother as my prayer warrior, I never felt a need to pray myself. My first awareness of God was during that storm and Mother's prayer, "God, stay Your hand," had saved us. I knew that as long as she was around, I had nothing to fear. As I grew older, my father's image as a stern, punishing, but loving teacher came into sharper focus. When I would see my mother and father together, it was her soft, gentle beauty and the apparent power she had over God and man that attracted me.

Coming from French and Cherokee stock, she had long, straight, black hair, which, when unbound, fell to her slender waist. When she stood beside my father, the crown of her head would come to his shoulders. Her dark eyes would flash with excitement and emotion while his hazel eyes would study everything with deliberate slowness. They seldom quarreled and when they did, more times than not, Mother would win. As a child, I always felt the glow of the love between them, but Mother always seemed to be the expressive source of that love.

Father was a handsome man and his hands were calloused from days and months and years of hard manual labor. His cotton rows were always the straightest. Our mules and other livestock were always the sleekest. His dignity was expressed by being the best farmer around. He provided us with food, clothing and shelter. We were never hungry or cold. When my brother Ernest died, one year before I was born, both my parents accepted Jesus, but father's taciturn nature kept him from being openly demonstrative of his deep love for God and for us. I loved my mother with a reverent passion and respected my father with a deep sense of duty. We were a church-going Baptist family, but for me, Mother was our connecting link with God. She was the one with prayer power, and I left all the praying up to her.

By the time I was 12, my father regarded me as big enough to do a man's work. He was exacting in his requirements and every time I hooked the mules to the cultivator, he let me know what he expected.

"Tommy, cotton's supposed to be grown in straight rows. That's the way I do it, and that's the way you're going to do it!"

My cotton rows were always as straight as his and when I "dirted" them up with the "middle-buster," they had the look of having been done by a mature farmer. The praise I gained from my father for a job well done was a reward that I prized highly. It instilled in me a driving need to excel in everything I did.

A year after the Armistice was signed, we left the Rose Creek farm and moved to a larger place just outside Casa, Arkansas. This meant moving into a new school and that gave me added incentive to be the best in everything.

I attended a four-room school located three miles over the ridge from our farm. Each room contained three grades and I managed to clear each room in just two years. My ears were always listening to the teacher when he was working with the grade ahead of me. It made my own work easier and allowed me to learn faster. My ambition wouldn't let me remain idle. I was the best in every sport and did the school janitor work after school. This didn't prevent me from running home in the spring and fall to help in the fields. In addition, I milked four cows every morning and night while my little brother fed the hogs and chickens. By helping each other, we made the workload lighter. We were a sharing family and that included the labor.

Under Father's watchful eye and in Mother's loving care, I grew to adolescent manhood. Graduating from high school at 16, I followed a decision I'd made, years before during the great flu epidemic, to become a professional baker.

During that dreadful time everyone in our family, except Mother and me, was down with the flu. We tended our own and ministered to everyone else as best we could. Mother would spend hours baking bread, which was all we could afford to do, and I would deliver gallons of our fresh milk and her bread to the families who couldn't do for themselves. The heartfelt gratitude of the people impressed me with the importance of bread and I became consumed with the desire to become a baker. When I announced my intentions to the family, they accepted my decision completely. It became their decision as well, and I was apprenticed to the Cox Baking Company in Little Rock. Mother and Father jointly asked only one condition to my accepting the job.

"Tommy," Mother said, with Father's nodded approval, "we want you here with us while you're learning your trade. You don't have to," she added, "but it would please us greatly."

Realizing that I'd no longer be able to help on the farm, I replied, "Then I'll give you my pay, and Mother can give me an allowance for the few things I'll be needing."

It was agreed, and I continued to live at home while starting my new career. My first assignment in the bakery was that of a bread wrapper. In addition, I cleaned and greased pans, swept the floors and did whatever the bakers didn't want to do. We had nine bakers in the shop and when the day was done I'd remain behind and practice on the machines. During the work shifts, I'd finish every assignment as fast as possible and volunteer to help the others if they'd teach me what I had to learn. My need to excel was a constant prod to my ambition, and my willingness to do additional work was gladly accepted by those around me. My foreman and the superintendent of the plant were both aware of my eagerness to learn and they encouraged me. In fact, my foreman took an almost fatherly pride in my progress.

A deep masculine voice, speaking in a clipped British accent over the aircraft's public address system, interrupted my thoughts.

"Good evening, ladies and gentlemen. This is your captain, and I'd like to welcome you aboard our nonstop flight to Houston, Texas. We'll be flying at 38,000 feet, and we've been assured of perfect weather all the way. In about three minutes, we'll pass over the coast of Ireland and your hostesses will begin serving dinner." He chuckled before adding, "Our departing temperature at Heathrow was a chilly 43 degrees, but Houston is preparing a warm welcome for us with a humid 91 degrees. You won't be needing your topcoats when you deplane. I hope you enjoy our flight."

Leaning forward, I peered down through the glass to catch a glimpse of the Irish coastline, but without a moon it was too dark to discern the difference between land and sea. A gentle touch on my shoulder turned my attention to the pretty, smock-clad, young lady standing in the aisle.

"Have you selected your dinner, Mr. Ashcraft?"

I hadn't even looked at the menu in the seat pocket and shook my head as I reached for it. Leaning forward, she smiled and murmured, "Captain Porter thinks you'll enjoy the filet mignon. It's from Hereford beef and very tender. Coming from Texas, you'll like it."

"That's what I'll have, then," I answered. "How did the captain know I was from Texas?"

Once again she smiled, showing dimples in each cheek. "Oh, Mr. Ashcraft, every member of the crew knows who you are." She dimpled even deeper and continued, "All of us heard you speak in Houston two months ago. Captain Porter has instructed that we take very good care of you."

"Is it possible to meet your captain?"

She bowed her head slightly and whispered, "I'll arrange it."

The broiled filet was marvelous as were the tiny whole carrots, baked potato and Caesar salad. I declined my dessert and settled back to enjoy a seemingly endless cup of rich dark coffee. The young lady's name was Shirley and she was following her captain's instructions. While warming up my coffee, she said, "When everyone settles down after the movie, Captain Porter would like you to join him in the lounge for a late-night snack."

I nodded my acceptance and thanked her.

Watching her work forward with her coffee pot, I decided against seeing the movie. There was a low hum of conversation in the cabin and the ever-present sound of rushing wind that comes with jet flying. Sipping from my cup, I allowed my thoughts to return to the Cox bakery in Little Rock and the seventeen-year-old boy I'd once been.

Jack, the bakery foreman, was a small, blond Irishman. He overcame his small stature with an overbearing, loud manner. His cocky attitude was aided by heavy drinking and swearing, but he must have recognized something in me that was different. At that time I was running eight miles a day, getting eight hours sleep and continuing the training schedule I'd set as a high school boxer. I loved to fight, and everyone at the bakery knew it. I was strong, alert and bright-eyed. Jack figured I needed very little more to make me a man and he set out to provide that missing element.

We worked nights at the bakery and I'd just finished stacking the loads for the morning's trucks when Jack sauntered up and leaned against one of the stacks. He'd just come from the ovens and his hair damply stuck to his gleaming forehead.

"Tommy," he asked, "do you go out to parties at all?"

I looked him up and down before answering. "Of course I do. We had a party at home last Sunday."

Mother played the organ, and folks would come over about once a month and we'd have a singin' all day and dinner on the ground. There'd be buggies and wagons tied up to our front fence and maybe 30 or 40 people having a good time. When I was much smaller, I thought chickens only had necks, backs and wings, because that's all we kids got to eat, but now I was in the drumstick-and-breast league. I told Jack about the party and watched a slow smile fill his pasty face.

"Well," he kind of half-growled, "my wife and I are having a party tomorrow night, and we'd sure like you to come. Can you make it?"

"Should I bring a date?" I asked.

"Naw," he casually answered. "We're just having a few people over, and we'd like to show you how a real man has a little fun."

I really felt relieved that he didn't want me to bring someone. The only girls I knew were from church and I wasn't sure they'd understand about the language Jack used most of the time. I told him I'd be there at eight o'clock. He winked and said, "Good boy, we'll try to show you how the other half has a good time."

Saturday night was our night off, and we didn't have to report for work until Sunday evening. As I finished the Friday night shift, it occurred to me that I'd never been to a party outside the school, church or home. The prospect of Jack's invitation was exciting. I'd be meeting strangers as an adult in a social atmosphere for the first time. I'd bought a new blue serge suit for my baptism the month before, and I decided that's what I'd wear to the party.

I'll never forget the pride I saw in my mother's eyes the Sunday I was baptized, and she said I looked grand in my new suit. To tell the truth, my baptism was her idea, but I figured it wouldn't do any harm and went along with it. She was still the one with the prayer power, and that was all that mattered to me. My relationship with God was completely tied to her. I hadn't even bothered to learn how to pray. The thought of worshiping God simply didn't occur to me.

Getting out of bed early Saturday afternoon, I announced that I was invited out that night. Mother and Dad were pleased and she wanted to know all about Jack. My brothers and sisters considered my invitation to mean that my foreman really liked me, and Dad counseled, "You'll have to be on your best behavior."

In telling Mother about Jack, I left out the parts about his drinking and swearing. I didn't lie to her, I just didn't tell her the bad things. I think she sensed what I didn't tell her, because that night as I was leaving the house, she followed me to the front door and said, "Let's have a word of prayer before you go."

She put her right hand on my head and lifted her left arm toward heaven. Her prayer was simple and to the point. From that day forward, every time I left the house for a social reason she'd stop me at the door and we'd pray the same prayer.

"Lord," she firmly said in my ear, "wherever he is, or whatever he's doing, if he isn't doing right don't let him have a good time."

Mother never told me not to do this or not to do that. There were never any "don'ts" from her. It was just that prayer. She was sure of her faith and gave it to us. The message of faith that she gave us kids wasn't complicated. "If you lead a clean life and do what's right," she would say, "then you'll go to heaven." I would look at my father and see the way he lived and did things—everything neat and clean, his cotton rows absolutely straight, all our stock healthy, harnesses and equipment always well oiled—and I would know that he agreed with Mother.

Going to church every Sunday and knowing what so many of the other people were doing and how they lived, made it hard for me to reconcile my parents' faith with the actions of others. I knew if they figured they were going to heaven, there were a lot of things I could do and still make it through the pearly gates. At 17, these were the questions my head kept asking my soul. When I was baptized, I'd accepted Jesus with my head and not my heart. The juices of youth were flowing in me and I secretly wanted some of the fun I saw the others enjoying. As I left the house for Jack's party, this was the attitude I took with me. Well, I found what I was looking for!

Entering Jack's house was like entering a different world. There were five couples sitting in his living room waiting for me to arrive. Jack was about 35, and his wife was just a few years younger. The others were all about the same age. I was flattered that these mature adults wanted a kid like me around. Jack made the introductions and then waved me into the kitchen. All the others followed us, with their drinks in their hands. I'd never had a drink stronger than sweet apple cider in my life, but that was about to end.

Sitting on the kitchen table were three gallon jugs of clear "white lightning." I knew what it was. I'd heard stories of how it was "stilled" back in the hill country. I knew it was illegal, and I knew what it could do to a man. My heart started beating faster just thinking about it. All the things I'd been taught in Sunday school about sin flashed in front of me. The others had been drinking before I arrived, and the gay laughter of the women excited me. They all seemed happy and carefree. The "white lightning" hadn't bothered them. Jack placed a hand on my shoulder and gently caressed the neck of one of the jugs with his other hand.

"Tommy, I'd like to introduce you to a good friend of mine," he said. "This is John Barleycorn, and it's about time you became acquainted with the joy he can give you."

Picking up the jug, he showed me how to hold it in the crook of an arm and swing the jug's mouth up to my lips. Taking a deep pull of the white liquid, he smacked his lips with a chuckle and handed it to me. I know I must have appeared awkward to those watching, but I tried to make it look like I'd done this sort of thing all my life. Trying not to smell what was in the jug, I took two big swallows and lowered it back to the table.

I couldn't breathe! My stomach was on fire! Tears were streaming down my cheeks! I must have been a sight to see, because everyone was laughing. With tear-filled eyes, I watched one of the women take a deep swig from her glass. She smiled and giggled as the liquor hit home. She was enjoying the foul stuff. I watched as Jack poured her a refill and then found the jug being pressed into my hands again. I couldn't refuse! It wouldn't be manly! I knew I could whip any of the men in the room and if they could hold "white lightning," so could I. Hoisting it to my lips, I took another pull. It went down smoother this time. I successfully resisted the temptation to gag and managed a tentative smile. Shouts of "Good boy" rang in my ears, and I lifted the jug again.

Warmth began spreading through my body. I caught myself

saying and doing things that I'd been afraid to express before. My inhibitions melted away. A glorious, lightheaded feeling grabbed my senses and demanded sustenance from the jug. I got myself a water glass and filled it to the brim with Jack's nodded approval. The other men were clapping me on the back and the laughing women were encouraging me. Phrases like, "Now you're a man," kept ringing in my ears.

I became the hit of the party. Everything I did brought on greater laughter. The women passed me from one to the other, rewarding me with kisses and squeezes. The scent of their perfume was overpowering. I could no longer smell the liquor, and the softness of their playful kisses opened a whole new world for me. My mind and imagination were in high gear. I was thinking the thoughts of a man! The flash of a silken leg took on new meaning. The accidental touch of a woman's hand was like electricity in my brain, sending living current through my body. I kept drinking but my glass was never empty.

My senses began to numb. The music on the Victrola all sounded the same. There were two, and sometimes three, of each person laughing at my foolishness. I'd get a thought and then forget what it was. Suddenly, I was no longer in control of myself. I was floating in blackness.

When color finally returned to my vision, my head felt as if it were being probed with hot wires. Even my hair hurt! A blinding light was streaming in through the bedroom window. I was in a strange room, on a strange bed. The pounding pain in my head refused to let my brain orient itself to my surroundings. I raised myself on my elbows, and the room began to spin. Falling back on the pillow, I slowly and painfully took stock of my condition.

Someone had removed my shoes, but I was still wearing my rumpled baptism suit. My tie was undone and the top buttons

of my shirt were loose. Carefully rolling to my side, I dimly
made out a framed photograph of Jack on the stand beside the
bed. I was in his bedroom, but it was daytime. The sun was
shining and I could hear birds singing outside. It occurred to me,
there was no other sound in the house! It was Sunday morning
and I was alone! What had happened to the others? Had I done
something terrible to them? Had my love for fighting come to
the surface with my drinking? Shuddering with guilt and pain, I
swung my legs over the side of the bed.

Sitting up, I waited for my dizziness to pass. When I felt I
could manage it, I stood. I dreaded walking to the bedroom
door. It was open, but I feared what I might find in the next
room. I leaned against the door frame with my eyes closed. The
pounding in my head was pure agony, but I was afraid to open
my eyes. Knowing I could put it off no longer, I looked.

The room was a shambles. Two chairs overturned. Drinking
glasses, some half full and others empty, stood everywhere.
Overturned ashtrays littered the floor, but there wasn't a living
soul in sight. Jack, his wife, all the others were gone! Hating
every step I had to take, I gingerly made my way to the kitchen.
My mouth felt like it was filled with dry cotton. A small trickle
of sweat ran down my spine. Once again, I stood in a doorway
with my eyes closed. Taking a deep breath, and using every
ounce of my strength, I forced them open.

Other than a filled ashtray on the kitchen table, the room
looked as I remembered it. The three gallon jugs were gone. The
cabinet door over the sink was open with a single clean glass
remaining on the shelf. My thirst became monumental, and I
staggered forward. Gulping down two full glasses of water, I
turned to face the room again. I was alone! I called out, but
received no answer!

The thought suddenly pressed down on me, so this is what

it's like to be a man. My head was splitting. Even the thought of food revolted my stomach. I took another glass of water and started looking for my shoes. They were neatly placed near the end of the couch in the living room. Getting them on my feet and laced was a seemingly impossible task, but I managed it. Without knowing what had happened to Jack and the others, I left the house.

# Chapter 2
## THE FOOLISH WISE

*"(He) wasted his substance with riotous living."*
**Luke 15:13**

While relaxing in my DC-10 seat, I must have dozed off for a few minutes because the air rushing past outside the window woke me. That sound had taken up a rhythm and my brain was supplying the lyrics. Without even thinking, I was humming "Amazing Grace" to the beat of the wind. The movie was over. The cabin lights had been dimmed. Conversation among the other passengers had softened and most of them were asleep. I was at peace with myself and I knew Jesus was in the seat beside me. All this time, the voice in my heart had been talking to Him.

Closing my eyes, I went back to the Cox Baking Company on Rock Street in Little Rock, Arkansas. It was a bright fall day and a gusty wind was blowing old newspapers along the street facing the loading dock. It was the end of the Sunday night shift and I hadn't talked to Jack during the entire evening. The relief I'd felt when I saw him at work, knowing I hadn't done some terrible thing at his party, was all I wanted from him. Preparing to leave for home, I heard his loud voice call from inside the bakery.

"Tommy, hold up. I want to talk to you. "

A sense of shame filled me. I'd gotten drunk at his house and passed out on his bed. I thought he wanted to rub it in and tell me I was still just a kid. He was grinning from ear to ear when he stepped outside. I mentally withdrew inside myself and prepared my defenses for the expected verbal onslaught, knowing that if he got too abusive I'd simply have to punch him out. Pulling up in front of me, he shook his head, as if with wonder, and softly said, "Man, can you hold your liquor!"

My mouth must have dropped open with surprise because he quickly added, "You put that stuff away in grand style, and you were the life of the party. But when you decide to take a nap, you're something else. All of a sudden you just stood up and announced that it was nap-time. You had your shoes off and were on the bed before any of us could talk you out of it."

At least I'd done it for myself and the women hadn't put me to bed. That thought made me feel a little less ashamed, but I still didn't know what had happened to the others.

"Why didn't you wake me when y'all left?" I asked.

"Oh, hey," he protested. "We didn't leave on our own."

"What happened?"

He glanced around and lowered his voice. "The police raided us. We all spent the night in jail! I knew it would really tear up your mother if you went to jail so I talked them out of taking you. After all, you weren't drinking when they arrived and there wasn't any booze in the room where you were sleeping. I told 'em that we'd never let you drink with us because you were too young."

"And they believed it?"

"Yeh," he laughed, "and that's why I wanted to talk to you." He shifted from one foot to the other before continuing. "Could you loan me 20 bucks? It took every cent I had to pay our fines and the wife wants me to stop at the store on the way home."

All I had on me was a $10 bill, and I gave it to him, saying, "Thanks for keeping me out of it, Jack. This is all I've got, but you're welcome to it."

He palmed the ten and mumbled his thanks. Our eyes met and in that instant, I knew he'd taught me a very valuable lesson. I didn't like the taste of liquor, but I loved the way it made me feel. In the future, I'd have to gauge my drinking to just enough to keep the glow. My self-confidence was completely restored by the time I got home. I've often wondered if my life would have been different if I'd gone to jail that night. I might have even fought the police had I been on my feet at the time of the arrest. In my drunken condition, I certainly wasn't in control of my actions. That was the first and last time I ever passed out while drinking. Jack's lesson had a lasting impression on me.

Liquor was illegal in any form and there was no such thing as a legal drinking age. I soon discovered that a boy of 17 could obtain all the booze he wanted as long as he could pay for it. The price for "white lightning" was a dollar a pint and the porters at any good hotel had access to an unlimited supply. The week that followed Jack's party was one of eager anticipation for me. I could hardly wait for Saturday night and the promise of euphoria that I knew I would find in a bottle of my own.

There was something else I learned at Jack's party and I couldn't shake it from my mind. Whiskey had a profound effect on my natural shyness. It allowed me to overcome my inhibitions with women and seemed to affect them the same way. This was marvelous for me because the stirring I'd begun feeling in manhood was demanding some form of expression. Booze was my gateway to sex, and I knew it.

I lost all interest in the girls I knew from school and church. They didn't drink. They were incomplete copies of my mother; not as perfect as Mother and, therefore, unworthy of my consideration. The girls I wanted were found at the public dances. They knew how to have a good time and they wore the clothes that allowed a man to see what he was getting. In three months' time, I'd learned all there was to know about finding such women. The Booster Club, a low-ceilinged dance hall in Little Rock, became my regular Saturday night hangout.

My working nights also gave me access to the pool halls during weekday afternoons. In addition, my natural ability as a fighter and wrestler brought me into contact with the "sporting crowd." Playing pool at a nickel a game didn't take much money, and I rapidly became a well-known "sport" in Little Rock.

Girls seemed to gravitate to me. My trim firm body and black wavy hair found an eager and responsive audience in the "ladies" at the Booster Club. With John Barleycorn backing me up, I soon learned I could fondle and squeeze to my young heart's content. The Saturday night I met Irene, she removed all sexual restrictions from my life and taught me the few remaining facts I needed to learn. She loved booze as much as I did, and I think probably for the same reasons.

Having been raised on a farm, I knew how life was conceived. Animal husbandry was no stranger to me. My father was an expert in the raising of livestock. I'd witnessed the mating of animals and the birth of their young. I knew the gestation periods of them all. As I observed, my father taught me about human birth. But it was Irene who taught me the joy of being a man with a woman. In her flashing green eyes, flaming red hair, eager lips and tender young body, I found a perfect match for the demanding desire created by my whiskey-inspired brain.

Irene added a new element to my life and created an

appetite for variety. She was the first of a long line of girls. At the time, I thought I was successful in keeping all this from my mother, but I know now that she was aware of my transgressions.

Every night of my life, while living at home, Mother kissed every one of us kids good night. Even when I was doing my first drinking and chasing, she continued this practice. I'd come home at three o'clock in the morning, get undressed and climb into bed, pull the quilt up over my mouth to hide the smell of whiskey and wait for her to come. She would always stop at the water bucket in the kitchen, take a cold sip from the dipper and quietly enter my room. Her cool lips would gently caress my forehead, and without saying a word, she'd leave.

The rich, ripe aroma of "white lightning," mixed with the remnants of cheap perfume, must have told her where I'd been and what I'd done. Lipstick stains on my clothes must have confirmed her suspicions. Every Saturday night, 52 weeks a year, I'd stand at our front door with a pint in my pocket, the keys to a "U-Drive-Em" car and wild date waiting, with Mother's hand on my head and whispered prayer in my ear. She knew what I was doing and trusted God to take care of me. Love was part of her faith, and I know she never judged me.

My work at the bakery progressed beautifully. Jack was proud of the man I'd become and gave me every opportunity to learn my trade. The other men also helped, and Mr. Broulette, the superintendent, was aware of my eagerness and ability to learn. His interest in me was exhibited by giving me assignments that contained some management responsibility. My personal life made no difference to him. In fact, I think he approved. In his eyes, it probably made me appear more mature and ready for the opportunities of manhood. My vocabulary had been enriched by the language of the older men around me and my independent, self-serving attitude fit their mold of masculine maturity.

In all things, my personal satisfaction came first. I felt totally justified in doing anything that gave me pleasure. In my young mind, I was the master of my life. Everything I did was done for my own self-centered benefit. It wasn't until years later that I realized that every man serves a master. Thinking I was in charge, I had surrendered and chosen to serve Satan. If and when I ever thought of God, He fell in the mold of my father. He was a God of "don'ts," exacting in His demands and quick to punish. By being my own master, I could escape His restrictions and add "fun" to my life.

I still continued to go to church with my parents and some of the men I'd see there were those I'd seen the night before. We'd exchange winks and smile at one another, knowing we were the "smart" ones in the congregation. After all, I thought, I've been baptized and saved like them. They don't think they're going to hell, and I'm as good as they are. I wasn't hurting anyone with the things I was doing and if they were sins, then they were small ones and whatever punishment I would receive would be correspondingly small. I credited my "good times" to myself and the resulting hangovers to a punishing God. If I ever really needed anything from the Lord, I knew my mother could get it for me.

A sweet, gentle voice was calling my name. Opening my eyes, I saw it was Shirley, my stewardess.

"Captain Porter would like you to join him for tea." She smiled and added, "I'm sorry if I wakened you. Were you sleeping?"

"No, my dear, I was very much awake." I pushed my seat lever and it snapped to an upright position. "Is the captain in the lounge?"

"Yes, sir," she replied and asked, "Would you prefer tea or coffee?"

Standing, I stepped sideways into the aisle. "Please make it coffee for me," I said and followed her forward. Entering the lounge, I found a small but unique group waiting for me.

Captain Porter was a shorter man than I'd expected. His well-groomed hair was turning grey and his clipped mustache was just a few shades darker. His pale blue eyes inspected me as he made the introductions.

"Mr. Ashcraft, you've already met Shirley, and these other two charming young ladies are Helen and Betty."

Both girls looked smashing in their neat airline uniforms. Helen's attractive black face beamed at me with confidence and she nodded her head at the mention of her name. Betty was a redhead and I couldn't help comparing her with the Irene of my memories. In appearance, they were a great deal alike. They were all drinking tea as Shirley served my coffee. We helped ourselves to a tray of crustless sandwiches. All the other passengers on the flight were asleep, but the girls left the galley curtain open so they could watch the call board in case someone signaled for service.

In the course of our conversation, I learned that Captain Porter had seen service in the R.A.F. during the last year of World War II. Helen was from South Africa and Betty was a former Sister (as nurses are called in England) at a London hospital. Shirley had been a part-time model before joining the airlines. It was apparent they knew more about me than I knew of them. They'd heard my testimony at a breakfast meeting of the Full Gospel Business Men's Fellowship International in Houston, according to Shirley. Pressing for information, I asked a general question.

"Can I assume we're all Christians?"

Nodding his head, Captain Porter answered first. "Helen and I are Church of England."

Betty's red curls bounced as she said, "I'm Methodist."

I glanced at Shirley and she dimpled, saying, "Lutheran."

"Then we can speak frankly," I added. "Has each of you accepted Jesus as the Lord of your lives?"

A frown creased Helen's forehead. "If I'm not flying, I attend church every Sunday."

Betty and Shirley volunteered the same information and my eyes rested on Captain Porter. He studied me a moment before answering, "I make it three or four times a year."

They hadn't answered my question and I asked it a different way. "Has each of you met Jesus and do you know Him as the living God?"

The captain felt my question was directed at him. "I'd go more often, but there are too many hypocrites in the churches." Leaning forward, he explained, "I know too many so-called Christians who don't practice what they preach."

"Captain," I asked, "do you refuse to drive your car on the highways for the same reason?" His eyebrows arched and I smiled before continuing. "I think you'll find those same hypocrites everywhere you go and if you separate yourself from God because of them, they've beaten you." Looking him straight in the eyes, I added, "But that isn't the answer to my question."

"What do you mean?" he bristled.

"Is Jesus your Master?"

"I have no master. I'm my own man," he replied. "I believe

there's a God, and that He'll come again to judge the living and the dead, but I'm as good as the next man and I'll take my chances."

Looking from one face to the other, I firmly observed, "Each of us serves a Master. There's no safe middle ground. We either serve God or we serve Satan. When Jesus comes, the degree of our service will be judged. He spelled it out for us in the third chapter of Revelation."

"How?" Betty demanded.

"Jesus said," I answered, "'I know thy works, that thou art neither cold nor hot: I would thou were cold or hot. So then because thou art lukewarm, and neither cold nor hot, I will spew thee out of my mouth.'"

"But I'm not an evil man," Captain Porter protested.

"None of us is evil," Shirley added.

"I may sin from time to time," Helen interjected, "but when I make my confession, I'm forgiven." Each of them nodded their agreement with this as the South African continued. "We all give to charity and do things to help others."

"I have no doubt of any of this," I conceded, "but good works alone will not save you." I extended my arms to include them all. "You must open your hearts to Jesus and ask Him to enter."

Saying, "That's all well and good for you," Captain Porter leaned back and picked up his tea. "But we have to earn a living, and having Jesus in our hearts won't make that any easier." He paused and grinned. "We've already broken company regulations by simply being involved in this conversation. Religious discussions while airborne are frowned upon; the psychologists claim that such activities can instill a fear of flying among our passengers." He sipped his tea. It was cold and he put his cup back on the tray.

I watched him get to his feet. I knew the cold tea had reminded him of how long he'd been off the flight deck, but I couldn't let him get away without one more shot from the Word.

"Nonetheless, Captain," I said while standing, "in the same chapter of Revelation, Jesus tells us, 'Behold, I stand at the door, and knock: if any man hear my voice, and open the door, I will come in to him, and will sup with him, and he with me.' You can still have Jesus in your heart and not violate your regulations."

His patient smile as he turned away told me that I had failed, but Shirley's soft voice at my ear was of another mind.

"You got to him, Mr. Ashcraft, just you wait and see." The others had dispersed into the darkened main cabin, and she confessed, "I accepted Jesus that morning in Houston and I've been working on them." She smiled up into my face, saying, "Thanks for the help."

I went back to my seat knowing that Jesus was smiling. He'd shown me that I wasn't the only one in the salvation business. Settling back, I tried to sleep, but all my senses were alert and I let my memory take over once again.

A turning point occurred in my life after I'd been working at the Cox Bakery for about two and a half years. I knew how to operate all the machines. I'd mixed the dough, made up the loaves, baked them and generally qualified myself as a master baker. The men I worked with recognized me as an equal. The limited amount of pastry baking we did was duck soup to me. My ambition and the need to excel had removed all the learning challenges available in the shop. One Friday night, near the end of the shift, Mr. Broulette called me into his small, glass-enclosed office. I entered with a sense of impatience, because I wanted no delay in getting off work that morning. I'd planned on getting my rental car and pint of whiskey for the Saturday dance on my way home. He had me close his office door before telling me to sit down in the chair directly in front of his cluttered desk.

The spring on his old swivel chair squeaked as he leaned back and said, "Tommy, you've learned all we can teach you here." He twisted sideways and stared at the flour company calendar on his east wall. "The next session of the American Institute of Baking in Chicago starts in three weeks, and we'd like you to attend."

My heart jumped into my throat with excitement. Graduating from the Institute's four-month course of study would qualify me for almost any job in the baking industry. I knew I'd still have to gain the experience to go with each job, but the Institute's certificate would mean ready acceptance of my qualifications. Afraid to trust my voice, I nodded my answer. Mr. Broulette chuckled at my obvious elation and added, "You've earned this, Tommy, and when you come back we'll have a better job waiting for you."

The bakery superintendent's words were still ringing in my ears as I walked over to the car rental agency. I was going to Chicago, and the future looked extremely bright. The good grades I'd always gotten in school were part of the accomplishment. My eagerness to learn and willingness to work had impressed the bakery owners and management. I'd done all this for myself. No one helped me. It was my talent that impressed them. I deserved all the credit. I was the master of my life!

Having such great news to celebrate, I bought two pints of "white lightning" from the hotel porter. This was going to be my night to howl. I'd be able to casually tell my friends about going to Chicago and how I'd have a big promotion waiting for me when I got back. They'd be able to see what an important man I was becoming. Irene, Janice, Mary and all the girls at the dance would look at me with greater admiration. Most important of all, Mother would have special reason to be proud of me.

When Mother said her prayer over me as I was leaving the house that night, I didn't even hear her words. I was so wrapped up in myself, and eager for the reaction of my friends, that I didn't have time for God. None of my good fortune was from Him, and at that moment in time, I was the most important person on earth. Oh, I planned to be nonchalant about it all and totally modest in the acceptance of my expected congratulations and admiration. I didn't realize God had something else in mind.

Beyond a casual remark such as, "Hey, that's great," nobody seemed impressed with my good news. Irene even started making a play for another guy. She had no intention of spending 16 Saturday nights home alone while I was away. My extra bottle of whiskey attracted the attention of several friends, and one of them even asked, "Why do you want to go to Chicago? Isn't Little Rock good enough for you?" My pride was stung. I managed to get into a couple of fights that night so the evening wasn't a total loss.

Outside of my family, and the men at the bakery who understood the importance of what was happening to me, no one seemed to care about my big break. All the "good old boys," my drinking buddies, actually seemed to resent it. A few of the girls, thinking I'd be a better marriage prospect when I returned, offered halfhearted congratulations, but nothing else. After all, they were like me, wrapped up in themselves. If something didn't directly affect them, it really wasn't important.

The train ride to Chicago was the first time in my life that I'd been more than a hundred miles from home. It gave me a chance to think, and I resolved to be the best student at the Institute. I'd show them all that Tom Ashcraft was a man to be respected and admired. By excelling in this, as I did in all things, my pride would be saved from the indifference of my friends.

# Chapter 3
# TWO LIVES HAVE I

*"And even as they did not like to retain God in their knowledge, God gave them over to a reprobate mind, to do those things which are not convenient."*

**Romans 1:28**

Keeping my resolve to excel was easy. I was graduated from the American Baking Institute at the top of a class of 150. My four months in Chicago ended with a party among my classmates that made Saturday night at the Booster Club seem like a Sunday school picnic. Al Capone controlled Chicago and everything a sinner could desire was readily at hand. They didn't have a regular source for "white lightning," but I soon learned to accept the refined taste of good Canadian whiskey. The results were the same, and that's all that mattered.

When I returned to Little Rock, my family welcomed me as a hero. Jack and the others at the bakery were delighted to see me. My foreman's elation was short-lived, however, when Mr. Broulette announced that I was being given his job. In less than three years, I'd completed my apprenticeship, attended the Institute and been promoted to bakery foreman. Jack left the company a few weeks later, but his gift, my love for liquor and easy women, remained.

I'd learned to smoke while I was away; cigarettes gave me the feeling of being more mature. I was the youngest man in my class, and I needed something, I thought, to make me appear older. Smoking also appealed to my sense of image. Every advertisement for cigarettes that I saw showed handsome men

in sexy situations with beautiful women. That's the way I saw
myself with a pure white cigarette between my fingers. I was a
foreman now, and I'd been to Chicago. I had an important
image to maintain. The fact that I was only 20 years old had to
be overcome. Of course, I didn't smoke at home. Mother
wouldn't like it!

Youth is a remarkable time of life. Bad habits, formed while
you're young, can assume great importance. The body can
accommodate the abuse, and physical recovery is generally
swift. The experience I'd had at Jack's party taught me how to
drink. I'd drink until I could just barely feel the edge of my hair;
when that got numb, I'd quit until I could feel my nose again.
Then I'd drink just enough to restore the numbness. This way, I
could always drive home without being too dizzy. I was playing
a very dangerous game. I could have wrecked the car and even
killed someone, but my pride told me I could handle it.

Mother's prayer must have worked to some extent. In all my
drinking, I never had an accident or was arrested. God must
have been looking after me, because I was doing everything I
could to make myself available to disaster. And Mother's
words, "Don't let him have a good time," always popped into
my throbbing head when I'd awaken after a night on the town.

With my increased earning capacity, I began to enjoy yet
another vice. The secret hotel card games caught my attention
through the "sports" at the pool hall. The thrill of taking a
chance, and pitting my wits and skill against others, excited me.
Winning was vital, but the challenge was even more important.
In my opinion, gambling was the sport of men, and I
considered myself a man. It was only a matter of time until my
Saturday activities included the horse races in nearby Hot
Springs, Arkansas. I had to fight my conscience over this, but
the excitement of the challenge won.

When I walked up to the betting window, the pressure of Mother's hand on my head and her whispered prayer in my ear was almost unbearable. I'd have to shake my head and forcibly change my thoughts in order to make a bet. On the days that I won, I chalked it up to my own cleverness, but when I lost, it was God answering my Mother's prayer. On those days, I'd promise myself, "never again," but I soon learned that these promises were easily broken.

The two years I spent as foreman of the Cox Baking Company were years of growing sin. I no longer limited my drinking to Saturday night, nor was I satisfied with such limited access to the girls I'd met. Working nights gave me every afternoon free and I soon found companions for my idle time. It's as if I were living two lives: one at home for my mother, and the other, outside for myself.

I was wallowing in a bottomless sea of self-indulgence. My pride in being a "man" and doing the things that I heard others just talk about became a source of great satisfaction. What I was doing also affected my brother.

When Frank graduated from high school, he came to me for a job. Mr. Broulette approved, and I hired him. He stroked my pride by wanting to be like me. I was his "big" brother, and he felt compelled to do whatever I did. We were hard workers, and Frank's alert mind soon justified his employment. We Ashcraft boys were considered "top hands" by all the bakers in Little Rock. We were known as "company men" and could be depended on to do things right. The exacting demands of our father taught us both to do our work well and to look out for the interests of our employer. Yet there I was, figuring I was my own master and serving myself with every foul practice I could acquire. My actions should have shown me who I was actually serving, but my stupid pride blinded me.

By allowing my natural leadership qualities to surface in the atmosphere of this pride, I surrounded myself with a willing and admiring audience. Shannon Curry, all Irish and skinny as a rail, was one of my closest friends and he loved to fight even more than I. We'd go to a Saturday night dance looking for trouble. It was all part of having a good time and, not being particular about whose girl we worked on, trouble wasn't hard to find. One evening, we spotted two vivacious creatures on the dance floor and nothing would do but that we separate them from their husbands.

Nudging me in the ribs with a sharp elbow, Shannon half shouted over the noise of the band, "I'd sure like some of that!"

Following the direction of his gaze, my eyes drank in the beauty of a slender, long-haired blonde with great hips and legs. She was laughing and talking over her partner's shoulder, to another girl, equally pretty in a dark-haired way. I assessed both and shouted back at Shannon, "The brunette's mine, you take the blonde."

It made no difference that they were married. We were full of whiskey, and that made them fair game for us. I was free to do whatever I wished as long as I could back it up with my fists. If the girl's husband didn't like my hands on his wife, he could give me something else to use them on. When the two couples danced near us, we cut in. The boys didn't like it, but as gentlemen they stepped aside.

My gal's body was everything it promised to be. My body was close enough to know. She seemed to be enjoying it as much as I was, and I guided her toward the other end of the room. Shannon and I had a jug in our rented car, and it was a matter of only minutes until I had her headed that way.

The light from the Booster Club sign allowed me to enjoy the graceful contours of her legs while she climbed into the back seat. My Irish friend and the blonde were already in the front. They passed the jug back. She took a pull of "white lightning," and, removing the bottle from her lips, handed it to me.

With fingers searching for the neck of her dress, I tilted it back and let Satan's fire flow into my body and inflame my brain. Her laughter, as she pushed my hand away, made her more enticing. I set the whiskey on the floor and gave her my full attention. She made a halfhearted protest, which I softened with a kiss. The heavy breathing from the front seat gave us a tempo to match. My hand caressed the smooth texture of her stockings and moved to the warmth of her thighs, when the car door was yanked open, and a roar of masculine anger filled the night air.

This was my element. Her husband didn't stand a chance. I came out of the car like a rocket! Shannon had his hands full with the other one's husband. We were right where we wanted to be: in a fight!

I humiliated him in front of his wife, as she had been humiliated by being caught with me. I was the physical master of them both and this salved my pride and glorified the life I'd chosen to live. I laughed as she helped her husband away, knowing she'd welcome me any afternoon that I wished to call while he was at work. Resolving to put the horns of a cuckold on him as soon as possible, I went back to my bottle. Straightening our clothes, Shannon and I watched them drive away. My girl's husband didn't see the smile she flashed at me, but I did. Going back to the dance, I picked up another charmer, and this time, I wasn't interrupted in the midst of my play.

My life had become a series of such incidents, spiced with gambling and lying. Knowing I could always punctuate my actions with brute force, it meant little to me that I might be destroying the lives of others in addition to my own. This was contrasted by the smug self-satisfaction I felt every Sunday when I sat beside my mother in church. Sometimes my girl would be there with her husband, and the meeting of our eyes would confirm a Wednesday afternoon date.

I was almost 22 when my routine of living changed. In order to better myself and make more money, I left the Cox Bakery and went to work for a high-class, home delivery bakery by the name of Frankie's. This gave me an opportunity to create products that went beyond bread and cinnamon rolls. Frankie's produced a complete line of fancy breads, cakes and pastries. My training at the American Baking Institute set me above the other men, and my new employer placed greater responsibility on me.

Frankie's owned and operated a fine cafeteria in downtown Little Rock, and it included a retail store for their products. One day during lunch, the gloss of long black hair and the flash of dark eyes caught my attention. She was perfectly beautiful, and I learned from my brother her name was Elizabeth. He'd had a couple of dates with her and was disappointed by her prudish attitude, but I could hardly wait to get next to her. Watching her move behind the counter while she waited on customers allowed me to appraise her petite and perfectly formed figure. She was graceful and seemed to glide on the balls of her lovely feet. The saucy French-maid's uniform set off her long, slender legs and delightfully trim ankles. She carried herself with the hauteur of a trained ballet dancer, which I later discovered she was.

Elizabeth became an obsession with me. She was included in my fantasies. Every time I saw her, I mentally undressed and caressed her, but it wasn't until one Saturday evening when Shannon and I were cruising for pickup dates that I finally got the nerve to approach her.

She was leaving a movie with a girlfriend when we pulled up beside them. She knew me because of my brother and wasn't offended when we stopped to talk. We asked them if they'd like to go to the dance, but they'd gone to the movie after their dancing class and were still wearing their gym clothes. They reluctantly agreed to go for a ride, and at last I was tucked away in the rumble seat of our rented Ford with the girl of my dreams.

I turned on the charm and gave my hands minds of their own, but Elizabeth wasn't having any of it. Her voice was low and sultry, but her resolve was firm.

"Tommy Ashcraft," she said, "there'll be no fooling around with me until we're married!"

That was the furthest thing from my mind. Women were supposed to be available to me and count themselves lucky if I accepted their offered favors. I knew she didn't mean it and continued to press for every advantage. She'd let me go just so far and I'd think I was about to score, when she'd shut down the game. I was becoming a basket case. The scent of her was driving me wild. I tried everything I could think of, but a polite kiss was as far as I got. Shannon wasn't doing any better with the girlfriend, either.

After that first date, I really set my sights on Elizabeth, and nothing was going to turn me away. I started renting a car by myself so that we could be alone. I thought this was the reason for her reluctance, but it wasn't. She really wanted to get married! About this time, the owner of the bakery moved her from the store to the plant. She became his secretary and now I was faced with seeing her while I worked. I'd watch her walk between the bread racks and dream of tumbling her into bed. She filled my thoughts day and night, and all the time, I was trying to play it cool and make her want me as much as I wanted her.

In her own way, she did want me. I'd find office memo pads with a sheet filled with her handwriting. Over and over she'd write, "Mrs. Thomas L. Ashcraft." I was getting the message loud and clear. There was only one way into her heart, and that was through the altar. This was a problem in more ways than one. The entire country was in the depths of the Great Depression and, even as the bakery superintendent, I was only making $27.50 per week. The management also had a policy against employees being married to one another, and we knew we couldn't make it on my salary alone.

Three weeks went by, and my sexual desire for Elizabeth grew stronger. We'd see each other every day and night. She held me off, and my desire continued to grow. She'd make hot steak sandwiches for me at her apartment and bring them over to the bakery. I was on fire for her, but economic conditions stood between us. We were selling the bread I made for four cents a loaf, and I simply couldn't see saddling myself with a wife. At the end of the third week we settled it.

With another couple as witnesses, we drove over to Lone Oak, Arkansas and had the justice of the peace give me legal access to her body. We tried to keep the wedding a secret, but after about four days our boss came to me and said, "I understand you and Elizabeth are married."

I admitted we were and added, "I suppose one of us is going to have to quit."

"No," he confessed, "you're both too valuable to me so I'm just going to overlook my rule as far as the two of you are concerned."

Elizabeth and I were married and our union was totally physical. The only joy we achieved was the satisfaction of our mutual lust. She was nothing like my mother. I called her a heathen because she was unchurched. Unlike me, she had attended religious services only a couple of times in her life. Mother was my pathway to God, but I knew Elizabeth wouldn't recognize the Lord if she saw Him in a red hat. I was the baptized, "good as anyone else" church-goer in our marriage. Whenever I thought of it, which wasn't often, I knew she had a long way to go before she'd be as good as I. I was the boss, and I let her know how superior I was in no uncertain terms.

We moved into an apartment, and for the first time in my life I was out from under the influence of my mother. This was a new degree of freedom for me, and I took advantage of it. Legally, Elizabeth belonged to me. She was my wife, but my monumental pride wouldn't let me accept the fact that I was bound to her in any way. As a man, I felt that I was still free to enjoy the fruits of the earth. Other than having a warm, submissive body available for my desires at almost any hour of the day or night, I felt no change in my life. This was the start of many long years of my taking and her giving. Her classic beauty was there for me to enjoy, and all I owed her in return was an occasional hug and a rub and a few kind words. I loved her, but my understanding of love was so incomplete that it hardly existed. What little love I had was for myself, and I consumed every ounce of it.

Leaning further back in my window seat, I looked out at the multitude of stars in the cloudless night sky. The recollection of my carnal nature had given me great discomfort. The pain of it bore down on me, and I silently wept. Without my really being aware of it, the voice in my heart softly said, "That ye love one another; as I have loved you." My tears continued to flow as I recalled how I had fought against that commandment from God.

# Chapter 4
# THE TOTALLED MAN

*"And about the time of her death the women that stood by her said unto her, Fear not; for thou hast borne a son. But she answered not, neither did she regard it."*

**I Samuel 4:20**

Young people today think they've discovered the new elixir of life when they joyously proclaim, "If it feels good, do it!" In truth, this selfishly satisfying attitude is as old as mankind. When Moses wrote the laws of Deuteronomy under the inspiration of God, he recognized this attitude in man and proscribed it. The prophet Isaiah defined this attitude with great detail in 701 B.C. and gave voice to the judgment of God, when he wrote:

"Yea, they are greedy dogs which can never have enough, and they are shepherds that cannot understand: they all look to their own way, everyone for his gain, from his quarter. Come ye, say they, I will fetch wine, and we will fill ourselves with strong drink; and tomorrow shall be as this day, and much more abundant. But the wicked are like the troubled sea, when it cannot rest, whose waters cast up mire and dirt. There is no peace, saith my God, to the wicked."

I didn't consider what I was doing to Elizabeth and myself as being wicked. I was being human. I was being a man, as God had made me. In all my church-going, if I'd listened to the preaching with my heart instead of my head, maybe I would have learned the difference. But I was judging myself by the acts of others. Surely, if they were saved as they proclaimed, then I too was saved. They were hearing the same "don't do this or don't do that" which I heard, and I was still running into them in places other than church. It never occurred to me that I didn't even know how to pray.

I'd never felt the need for prayer. Mother knew what was good for me and she took care of it. When God taught me the fallacy of this, I didn't have brains enough to learn the lesson! I prided myself on my intelligence and ability to be the best in whatever I did, but even the pain of this lesson didn't make an impression on me.

Elizabeth and I had been married for about a year when our son Tommy was born. The occasion gave me the bragging rights to say, "I'm a complete man." Beyond that, fatherhood held little meaning. I was still the same person. My drinking continued to increase. I still demanded time to do my own thing. After all, I was a sportsman. Hunting, fishing, gambling, wenching, lying, smoking and drinking were the important things in my life, because they satisfied my selfish nature. The first warning signs of my lesson to come didn't get my attention. Over a period of about two years, I began to experience flashes of sharp pain in my lower abdomen on the left side. Time after time, I'd go to the doctor thinking it was appendicitis, but the tests showed nothing. The pain would go away, and for a time it would be forgotten. My mother was also feeling signs of physical weakness and failing. She'd undergone serious surgery three times and recovered. Each time she suffered, I experienced fear that I might lose her. This fear was real because she was the one person, other than myself, that I truly loved. Each time she went under the knife, I lived in that fear, but her powerful faith always brought her back. The weekend of my own trial made the fact of her faith even stronger in my mind.

In keeping with my lifestyle, I grandly announced a fishing

trip with the boys. Elizabeth's negative reaction to such plans didn't surprise me. She wasn't interested in the thing that I enjoyed. Her selfish interest was limited to having me available to do the things she wanted done. I'd heard the preacher say, "Wives, be submitted unto your husbands," and that's exactly the way I was going to keep her. She was a pagan, and I was baptized! For this reason alone, she had to bend to my will! She didn't like having me come home dirty and drunk, but that was my right and she'd have to live with it!

I went fishing with the boys. We took a lot of beer and whiskey, but very little bait. When we ran out of ice for the beer, we drank it warm. In spite of ourselves, we caught fish and when we ran out of things to drink, we brought them home. I roared my way into the house and staggered to the kitchen. Throwing my catch in the sink, I proceeded to clean them, unaware that Elizabeth had followed me through the kitchen door.

"I'm not going to cook them for you," she screamed.

"Yes, you are," I growled over my shoulder. "You're going to cook 'em and serve 'em to me because I'm hungry."

Her answer was a flying dish that smashed on the cabinet over my head. Turning to face her, I saw the fury of hell flashing in her beautiful dark eyes. Ducking under the next dish, I heard it crash as I lurched forward. "Get out of the kitchen!" I ordered. She stopped me with a third dish that grazed my shoulder and shattered on the floor behind me.

Whirling in anger, she shouted, "Go to hell!" and slammed the kitchen door behind her.

In my befuddled, drunken daze, I wanted to chase her and beat her into submission, but my pride chose another alternative. Going back to the sink, I loudly proclaimed, "I don't need her. I'll fix these fish myself, and I'll eat every damned one of them."

I fried them in a pan full of oil and ate them with a gusto spawned in hell. I stuffed them down inside me on top of all that warm beer and whiskey. Reveling in the pleasure of my anger, I left the carnage of my gluttony for her to clean up and, taking a fresh beer from the refrigerator, manfully stomped my way to bed.

"I'll straighten you out in the morning," I declared, more to myself than to her, as I fell asleep.

At four o'clock in the morning, getting Elizabeth straightened out was the farthest thought from my mind. I couldn't get myself straightened out. I was curled up in a ball of agony. My lower stomach was on fire, and tendrils of pain filled every nerve in my body. Elizabeth reacted with love, but I was unaware of it. She called the doctor and tried to comfort me. When he arrived, I was almost out of it. My pain and temperature were at their zenith.

Not wanting to wait for an ambulance, and in the fear that I was dying, the doctor raced me to the hospital in his own car. Once again all tests showed nothing wrong with me, and six other doctors were called in for consultation. They decided to perform an exploratory operation to see what they could find. I agreed and they put me under.

They found my gangrenous appendix embedded in a hard ball of fat. Peritonitis was already raging inside me. They removed the source of my pain and washed me out as best they could. Not believing that I'd live, they clamped me closed, saying, "We'll sew him up if he survives!"

When I was placed in intensive care, my mother took up her station at the foot of my bed. For five days, I wavered between life and death. Mother prayed constantly for my healing, and when everyone but her was about to give up, my body expelled its poison. As I lay in a pool of my own filth, my temperature broke and it was confirmed that I'd live. Once again, the power of Mother's prayers had saved me. Without her, I'd have surely died.

My recovery was slow and my brush with death hadn't changed any of my thinking. Just as it had been when I was a little boy and Mother had shouted over the wind, "God, stay Your hand!", it was her faith and prayers that held the power. Elizabeth was constantly with me, serving as my nurse at home, but Mother had been worthy; she'd performed the miracle. Once I was back on my feet, I immediately reverted to the life I'd lived before. I didn't even thank God for my healing. Whatever thanks I had to offer was included in the love and devotion I gave to my mother. I didn't know there was still more to come in the lesson God was teaching me. Nor did I know that my pride was too great for me to learn.

Once I was back at work, I found it easy to fall into the pattern of my old life. My eyes caressed every girl I saw and my drinking continued to grow. Weeks passed and became months. My married life didn't improve, and Elizabeth's resentment increased. It would have been plain to any thinking man that I was on a sliding path of moral degradation, but in my opinion I was merely being the man I was intended to be. Early one morning, my brother came to work late with news that sharply jarred my complacency.

I knew from the expression on his face that something was wrong, and the alarm in his voice confirmed it. "Tom, Mother is seriously ill. She wants all of us to come home."

Elizabeth was at home with our young son, and she was once again pregnant. I didn't want to bother her. I really didn't consider her as part of my personal family. Frank insisted that we call Alpha and Ann, our two oldest sisters, and tell them we'd be by to pick them up. Our younger sister Jo was living at home with Frank, and she was already there.

None of us said very much during the ten-mile drive out to the house. Each of us, in his own way, was thinking of Mother. She'd been sick twice before and had recovered, so in my mind I knew, with her closeness to God, she'd recover again. The grim set of Dad's face when I entered the house told me this time was different. He looked drawn and his eyes were filled with pain.

"The doctor's in with her now," he softly said, while leading the five of us toward the bedroom door.

I'll never forget the scene that greeted me when I entered that room. Mother looked extremely small lying in her bed. One of the quilts she'd made was pulled up around her. Her entire right side was paralyzed. Her left eye was closed, but her right eye was open, staring unblinkingly at the ceiling overhead. At first she seemed unaware of us and my heart jumped with fear. We'd come too late, and she was already gone. Her tongue was hanging out, and when it slowly returned to her mouth, I knew she was still alive. Suddenly I could see how gray her hair had turned and how frail this mighty woman of God had become. We could hardly hear her voice when she spoke.

"Come closer," she said. We gathered around the bed in silence. The effort it took for her to speak filled me with pain. "I've asked God to let me live until all of you are grown," she softly murmured, "and He's done that." She paused as if to gain strength. "Now I'm asking God not to let one of you be lost."

At that time, not one of us really knew Jesus. We'd all been baptized, and we went to church regularly. I looked around at each face without understanding what Mother was really saying. We were Christians, as good as many and better than some. My two oldest sisters were married to good Christian men. Jo and Frank, by living at home, had never totally escaped from Mother's influence. I'd even been baptized twice, so there was no doubt about my having been saved. I simply couldn't understand Mother's concern.

We started to assure Mother of our goodness, but the doctor shushed us and ushered us out of the room. Frank and the girls gathered around Dad to console him, and I walked out on the porch to have a cigarette. Her words still echoed in my brain, and I felt the need to be alone. The one person on earth that I loved more than life itself was dying, and I was helpless to do anything about it. Going to the car, I got in and drove a short distance from the house.

Sitting quietly beside the road, I put my head down on the steering wheel and cried. She'd prayed for me when I was near death, and God had honored her prayers. Now, when she needed my prayers, I didn't even know how to pray. I tried, but my spirit wouldn't respond. All my life she'd been my pathway to God, and I knew He wouldn't listen to anything I had to say. My pride wouldn't let me beg for His divine intervention. Suddenly, a harsh pain entered my heart. I started the car. I had to get back to the house!

With tears streaming down my face, I ran into the house, but I was too late. Mother was gone. My grief became so terrible. I turned away and tried to hide the terror in my heart. Blindly, I got outside and headed for the barn. Getting as far as Dad's corn crib, I crawled inside and lay on the floor.

My heart was shattered by unbearable anguish. In my pain, I was angry at God. He'd taken her away from me. He'd stolen my prayer warrior. He'd claimed my teacher. The memory of all the evil I'd done in my life flooded in on me. I struck back in the only way I knew how. The fists that had served me so well in my sin now served me in my anger. I pounded the crib floor and the ears of corn. I was frustrated and felt humiliated by my helplessness. I was Tom Ashcraft, and God had betrayed me!

Frank came and pulled me from the crib. He helped me walk off my despair and outrage. Dad needed us all. My selfishness wouldn't let me admit it, but his loss had been greater than mine.

After the funeral, I knew I couldn't remain in Arkansas. Too many memories haunted me. Everywhere I looked, I saw something of Mother. Seeing one of her friends would give me pain. Just going in a store where she had shopped made me remember her sweet voice. I had to get away.

Elizabeth's mother and father had moved to Houston, and sensing the torment I was suffering, she suggested that we pay them a visit. The bakery owner gladly gave me time off and I loaded my little family in our 1937 Chevrolet and we headed for Texas. After our second such visit, I knew that Texas and I agreed with each other, and on our third visit, I took some action to make it permanent. Finding a shopping center under construction, I leased the space for a small bakery of my own.

The prospect of being my own boss was exciting and when we returned to Arkansas, I was impatient to get moved. Being the superintendent at Frankie's was a good job, and with Frank as my bakery foreman, we'd made a good team. When I told my employer of my plans, he wished me well and promoted Frank to my job.

Saying goodbye to Dad and my sisters wasn't easy, but it wasn't as if we were moving to the end of the earth. They promised to visit often, and I knew we'd come back from time to time. Two years after our first visit to Houston, we made the move, and I left all my unpleasant memories of Mother's death behind me. I remember her now as she was when I was growing up, with her beautiful, long black hair and the warmth of her soft, quiet smile.

It was early May, 1939, when we arrived in Houston. I put our life savings into the bakery and established Elizabeth, Tommy Jr., and Shirley, my sweet little daughter, in a rented house. From a financial standpoint, it was touch-and-go at the start, but the quality of our products began to build the business and my reputation.

Later that year, the owner of the Chocolate Shop Pie Company on the north side of Houston asked me to come to work for him. He wanted me to manage his operation, and I accepted. With income from two sources, the pie company and my own bakery, life began looking pretty good. I had money to do the things I enjoyed doing. It didn't take me long to find the type of friends I wanted. My drinking and gambling increased.

I'd been baptized the third time before we left Little Rock. Elizabeth had shared this last experience with me and after getting settled in Houston, we joined the biggest Baptist church in town. I knew all the elders and they knew me. I'd often run into them, both while working and playing. It seemed to reassure me that I was doing okay when I'd see some of the church leaders doing the same things. "If they're saved," I'd say to myself, "then I'm saved too."

This hypocrisy wasn't limited to my Baptist friends. There were prominent Methodists, Episcopalians, Lutherans and Roman Catholics in the pack. We were all "good" church-going folks who just loved to have a "good" time. It never occurred to me what this fun-loving, hypocritical attitude was doing to my wife.

Right after I'd been offered the superintendent's job with the Hinke-Pillott Bakeries, and I'd begun holding down three jobs at the same time, we bought our first home. It was in a nice, socially acceptable part of town, and I thought it represented a degree of my success. Being able to entertain my friends there was also part of my great accomplishment. Elizabeth and the children would have to endure my drunken, smoke-filled poker parties. They'd see and hear our "manly" activities and all the "good old boys" thought Elizabeth was a sweet, submissive, "purty little thing" who'd do anything I told her. They didn't see or hear us the other times.

I'd come home at all hours, so drunk that I couldn't find my keys, and have to wake her to get in. She didn't want me in and I'd have to throw rocks at the windows and stagger around yelling until the whole neighborhood was up and awake. Lights would go on, windows would fly up and voices would join mine yelling, "For Pete's sake, let the squarehead in so we can get some sleep!"

Sometimes when I did get in the house, I wasn't sure it was the right thing. She'd meet me with a cold fury that I found extremely difficult to handle. In fact, I didn't handle it. I rode roughshod over it. I'd take my high-and-mighty, lord-of-the-manor attitude and jam my conduct right down her throat! At least, that's what I thought I did. After all, Elizabeth wasn't the strong prayer warrior my mother'd been. She'd only been baptized once, and she sure didn't believe the Bible.

I didn't know much about the Bible, either, but I did know that my wife wasn't the silent, submissive type that the apostle Paul recommended. She could yell louder than I and bounce a plate off my head at the least little provocation. I could always rationalize and justify the things I did, but when Elizabeth objected, she was simply being mean, bullheaded and ungrateful.

After all, I deserved a little fun and relaxation. I was working three jobs just to give her the good life. The country was at war, and I was supplying "our boys" with good wholesome bread. I was classified as "essential to the war effort" and deferred from the draft. Even the government recognized the importance of the work I was doing, but Elizabeth couldn't see or understand this. Even after I sold my bakery and quit the pie company job so that I could apply myself completely to the Hinke-Pillott operation, she didn't understand what an important man I was. I'd try to relax a little bit after a long, hard day, and she'd resent it. She even expected me to come home and toady around her and the kids.

When I'd wake up with a splitting head after a night on the town and waking the neighbors to get in the house, she'd never give me any sympathy. She'd always find some reason to slam some pots and pans around and berate me for my conduct. Instead of sweetly fixing me a good breakfast and a healing "Bloody Mary," she'd start in with a snide "I hope you're proud of yourself!"

I'd ignore her sarcasm, and she'd hit me with "Why can't you be like other men and come home sober once in awhile?" Or she might say, "What do you think the neighbors think this morning?" Then, raising her voice a couple of octaves, she'd tell me what they were thinking. "Ashcraft came home drunk again last night. How does that poor woman stand him?"

After taking all I could of this, I cut loose. "Shut up, woman! This is my house, and I'll do as I damned well please! I'm paying all the bills around here, and you'll take whatever I dish out!"

With that, she'd usually sail my breakfast across the room, aimed right for my head and storm out with all her flags flying. By the time I'd leave to go to work, my blood pressure would be at its usual high peak. My stomach would be in a turmoil, and my mood would be set for the day. I could hardly wait for lunch time when I could have a few belts and start feeling good again. By quitting time, I'd really be rolling and ready for another night of fun with the people who knew how important I was.

From a financial standpoint, I had the world by the tail. I was making good money. Mr. Sutherlund, the president of Hinke-Pillott, was a fellow alcoholic and my friend. The bakery division of the company, under my supervision, had become profitable for the first time, and I was offered a vice presidency. I refused because it would mean giving up my profit-sharing bonus. As it was, my annual bonus always paid for the stock options I was allowed and as the years passed, I was accumulating a sizable block at no direct cost to me.

One evening in March of 1944, I came home relatively sober and early. Elizabeth met me at the door with a proposition. It was the first time since moving to Houston that she and I agreed on anything. "Tom," she seriously said, "I want a divorce. I can't take any more of the crap you're giving me. I'll take the children since it's obvious you don't want them."

"Okay," I grandly agreed, "if that's what you want, I'm all for it."

I really didn't want a divorce, but my pride wouldn't let me admit it. We also agreed to see a lawyer and work out the details for an uncontested break in our marriage. After checking with a few friends, who'd had experience with this sort of thing, we agreed on an attorney and made an appointment.

During the few days' wait, before our meeting with the attorney, I had a chance really to think about what we were doing. There'd never been a divorce in my family, and I didn't want to be the first. I didn't know I loved Elizabeth, but I knew I liked her in a perverse sort of a way. She was a good housekeeper. She was the mother of my children. Our sex life, whenever I was sober enough to be pleasant, was fine. I knew there was something missing from our marriage, but I couldn't put my finger on it.

I'd always been a good provider. It was just her unwillingness to accept my rights as a man. It was amazing how much our lives calmed down during that few days' wait. The strain of one dominating the other was gone, but it took the confrontation with the attorney to get my attention.

We went to his office, and he talked to Elizabeth alone for about 15 minutes. She came out, and I went in. He listened to my side of the story and then met with us together. His opening remarks brought me up sharply.

"Mr. Ashcraft, as I see it, you haven't a leg to stand on. Your wife is going to get everything: the car, the house and your salary. The court may grant you enough for board and room, but that's about all."

Well, I hit the ceiling and came down snarling. Elizabeth wasn't silent either. We went at each other with everything we could lay our tongues to. The lawyer finally stepped in and shut us up.

"Look," he said, "you two aren't going to agree on anything. Why don't you go home and try it again for another 30 days? If you still feel that a divorce is the only solution, you can then come back, and I'll set it up."

He was really a good man, and he was trying to keep us together. Those 30 days were among the longest I'd ever spent. We talked to each other through the children. Even in the same room, I'd tell Tommy Jr. to tell his mother something for me and she'd reply in the same manner. I was trying to be the type of man I thought she wanted. I didn't go out every night, but there were some social obligations that I had to keep if I still wanted my friends. After all, I figured, they're all I'll have left after the divorce.

Our second visit to the lawyer was almost a repeat of the first. Once more, he sent us out for another 30 days. He wasn't

a godly man, but he knew the true meaning of divorce and was
trying to help us avoid it.

On our third visit, he asked, "Do you folks belong to a
church?"

"Yes," I indignantly replied. "We belong to the biggest church
in town."

"How often do you attend?"

"Whenever we need it," I answered.

He looked at me in silence for several minutes before saying,
"Well, it isn't doing you much good. Why don't you try a
different church?"

"Look," I protested, "I've been baptized three times! If
someone needs churching around here, it's Elizabeth."

I'll never forget his smile as he said, "Nonetheless, I think you
both better try another one. I'm Jewish, but I know and respect
a lot of good Christians, and you two sure aren't like them."

We left his office for another 30 days, after promising to
follow his suggestion. On the way home, you could have cut
the silence in our car with a dull knife. I was seething inside. I
was as good a Christian as anyone else. It was Elizabeth who
needed the Lord, and I told her so.

"Damn it, woman, if you'd study the Bible you'd find out
who's wrong in our marriage. I'm a good Christian, and you're
still pagan!"

She was sitting as far away from me as she could get, but I
heard her loud and clear. "If you're an example of a good
Christian, then I don't want any part of it." Facing me, she
added, "If I have to do the things you do to be acceptable to
God, then He's not the God I think He is, and you can have
Him."

That set me to thinking, and I silently agreed to try another
church. I told her to find a church close by the house and we'd

try it the next Sunday. She reluctantly agreed. When we turned into our neighborhood, we drove right past a little white Pentecostal church and she said, 'There it is. That's the one we'll try."

# Chapter 5
# SHOCKED OUT OF MY SOCKS

*"He that hath ears to hear, let him hear."*
**Matthew 11:15**

I must have dozed off once again. The pitch of the engines changed slightly and woke me. Looking out the aircraft window, I couldn't distinguish any detail of the ocean below. Everything looked black. I headed for the restroom.

The memory of our "almost" divorce had stirred thoughts toward the thousands of people who have faced or will face a similar situation. So many of them enter marriage on the same basis as I did, and it's no wonder that our divorce rate is climbing. We let our carnal natures take over and run our lives. Looking in the restroom mirror, I saw the face of a grateful man. Elizabeth would be waiting for me at the Houston airport only because Jesus had entered our lives.

The Sunday morning after our third trip to the attorney, Elizabeth rolled out of bed with the bit in her teeth. "You'd better get moving if we're going to church," she said. "I called them yesterday and their services start at 10 o'clock."

Still half asleep, I muttered, "Are you sure we want to go to a Pentecostal church?"

"Do you have a better suggestion?" she snapped. "It's close by, and it's a nice looking building."

"I don't understand why that lawyer wants us to change churches." I rolled onto my side and faced her. "I'm sure our good old Baptist church is as good as any of 'em."

"Make up your mind," she pressed. "If we're going anywhere you better get started."

"Okay," I agreed and swung my legs out of bed. "Let's try that pretty little Methodist church we always pass on the way downtown."

We did some very fancy "church-hopping" for the next four or five weeks, but I didn't think we were getting anything out of our efforts. I even considered going to a Roman Catholic church, but I knew too many people who figured their confessions allowed them to continue sinning, and that didn't seem right to me. The fact that I was judging them didn't seem important. In any event, our marriage wasn't improving, and I was about to give up and return to the attorney.

Coming home early one afternoon, I found Elizabeth visiting with her Aunt Oma in our living room. When I'd been introduced to Oma at one of the family gatherings, they'd told me as an aside that she was a little "peculiar" in a "churchy" sort of way. She was what they called a "Pentecostal Christian." That didn't mean much to me, and I viewed her as just another one of Elizabeth's relatives. After greeting her, I sat down with them and listened.

Oma reminded me of my mother. She seemed to have a strong, positive relationship with God. Like my mother, Oma didn't use makeup, and she wore her hair up on top of her head. Her flowered dress was worn high on her neck, and there was a serene sense of peace and modesty about her. She was a sweet-looking woman. Being in her late fifties, Oma felt the authority of her age, and her first question to me demonstrated this attitude.

"Honey, are you a Christian?"

I figured the last person in the world who could question me about my Christianity was a member of Elizabeth's family. I matter-of-factly told her, "I have been baptized three times in water, and that's enough."

"I didn't ask you that," she replied. "I want to know if you know the Lord and the forgiveness of sins."

The tone of her voice carried the positive authority of her own deep faith, and I felt like I was being put on trial. My pride rebelled, but that didn't stop her.

"If you died right now," she asked, "would you go to heaven?"

She'd hit the question I had about faith right on the head. All my life, I'd questioned the actual existence of both heaven and hell. Hitting my personal problem with faith was too much for me.

"Listen," I said while getting to my feet, "I don't need some old lady coming around here bugging me about religion! This is my house, and I don't have to take any crap here! I want you to leave, and don't bother about coming back!"

Elizabeth was upset, but Oma didn't even blink an eye. She got up and marched out without another word. I thought I'd seen the last of her, but the Lord had other plans. Aunt Oma came back the following week and took Elizabeth to a prayer meeting at her Pentecostal church. This was the beginning of my salvation, but I didn't know it.

A gentle hostility existed between Elizabeth and me for the next few days. We shared the house and the children, but little else. There were no great changes taking place in my life and as far as I could·see, nothing was changing with her, but Oma and her fellow Christians were at work.

Coming home early without stopping for my usual drinks one Thursday afternoon, I realized that I didn't have my house keys. Knowing this would mean having a hassle just to get in the house, I wasn't overjoyed with my prospects. At least it wasn't the middle of the night, and I wouldn't have to wake the neighbors. Elizabeth shocked me right out of my socks.

When I rang the doorbell, she opened it with a smile and greeted me with a kiss. Her kisses had been few and far between lately, and this reception was a pleasant surprise. Her first words completely threw me:

"Oh, Daddy, I'm glad you're home. I've got a nice hot supper ready for you."

Now, she'd called me a lot of things, but the word "Daddy" hadn't been used in years. And having a hot supper ready for me was something that just hadn't been happening since the first year of our marriage. Of course, I really couldn't blame her for that because I normally wasn't too interested in a hot supper at three or four o'clock in the morning.

Not being able to believe my eyes and ears, I followed her through the house in dumb amazement. She'd done everything in the world to me except treat me nice, and I figured she might be trying this in final desperation, but there was something else about her that I couldn't understand. She looked happy!

"Now, Daddy," she sweetly said, "I want you to sit down at the kitchen table and have a cup of coffee while I finish preparing dinner."

I hadn't said a word and all this was happening to *me!* She looked great. Her hair was nicely fixed, and she was wearing a pretty red-and-white print dress. There wasn't anger in her voice. Her eyes shone with joy. She was actually half-singing and humming a little song about Jesus. The more I watched her, the more she amazed me. I'd drink about half my cup of coffee, and she'd refill it. She was cooing over me and using little terms of endearment that I hadn't heard in years. By the time supper was ready, I was convinced that I was either dreaming or I'd lost all sense of reality.

The dinner was fantastic. Elizabeth, the kids and I were all seated at the table at the same time. If one of our neighbors had peeked through the window, he'd have wondered if some new people had moved into the neighborhood. She even asked me how my day had gone and seemed interested in my answers. Elizabeth had to be up to something, but I couldn't figure out what it was. Once dinner was over, she gave me a hint of what was to come.

"Daddy, I want to talk to you."

Wiping my mouth with my napkin, I said, "Okay, what do you want to talk about?"

She sent the children out to play and suggested that we go into the living room. I followed her and took an easy chair opposite hers. I didn't know what to expect, but I knew she was planning a good one, and my defenses were automatically up. It's funny when I think of it now, but I actually checked the items in the room to see how many objects were at hand which she could throw at me. I completely overlooked the small black book she was opening in her lap. When she held it up, I could see that it was a New Testament.

"Daddy," she murmured, "I want to read something to you."

Oh boy, I thought, this pagan wife of mine is going to read the Bible. I didn't know anything about the Bible. I'd never read it, but I'd been baptized three times in water, and Mother's old Bible was upstairs in one of my bottom dresser drawers. Whenever I wanted to impress anyone with my religiosity, I always showed them Mother's old, dearly worn book of Holy Scripture. At least then they knew that I came from a Bible-reading family.

Even when I went to church, I never listened to the sermons or the teachings. After all, I was already a member of the congregation. I'd pitch all the preacher's words on back to someone who needed them. The idea of sitting still while my wife read the Bible to me was almost repugnant. What did she know about God? I was the one who had pledged $10 a month to God, not her. Up until that fool attorney had interfered, I'd been attending a church that had 120 deacons. I'd even got drunk with several of them. If they were saved, so was I. What business does she have reading me the Bible?

We'd been sitting there for almost two hours without an argument. She was reading scripture, and it suddenly dawned on me that this was a miracle! We still hadn't had an argument by 11 o'clock. *Will the wonders of God never cease?* In spite of all her sweetness, however, a resentment was growing in my heart. I was actually angry when I went to bed that night.

All the next day my resentment grew. I'd spent an entire evening listening to Elizabeth read, and it bugged me. She didn't know anything about the Bible. Was she trying to prove that she was more religious than I? Well, I decided, I'll show her a thing or two. Who does she think she's dealing with—some "Johnnie-come-lately" to this God business?

I didn't stop for drinks that night. I headed straight for home. Entering the house with a flourish, I proclaimed, "Hurry up and let's get dinner over with, and then let's get in there and get with it with that Bible."

Once again, I went to bed angry at 11 o'clock. We'd spent the entire time reading the Bible, and every time I'd open my mouth to explain something to her, she'd correct me right from the Book. I couldn't understand what was happening to her. She had no business knowing the Bible better than I did. I was the godly one in the family, not her. Not only that, but all the time she was acting like she loved me! She must spend the entire day reading and rereading the Bible, I thought.

At the office the next day, I could hardly do my work because of her and that Bible reading. It was getting to me! Once again, I got home on time. We'd barely finished dinner when I said, "Okay, now let's get back to our Bible reading." Pushing my chair away from the table, I stood and added, "Tonight, I'm going to prove that you're wrong."

Elizabeth dazzled me with footwork! That night she skipped from one book of the Bible to another, reading scriptures about salvation and everlasting life. I didn't stand a chance against what God was leading her to read to me, but I didn't have brains enough to know that He was involved. Once again, I went to bed angry.

My days were becoming a routine of frustration. I'd smoke three packs of cigarettes and I'd drink at lunch, but when quitting time rolled around, I was ready to do Bible battle again, and I'd head straight home. On this fourth night, she met me at the door with a great big kiss and led the way back to the kitchen. I was bound and determined to prove my Bible superiority, but passing the piano, I stopped to snub out a cigarette in the ashtray. There beside the ashtray was an open copy of the New Testament. Looking around the house, I found open copies all over. Each copy was open to a different book and chapter with particular verses underlined. I couldn't resist reading what she'd marked for me. Everywhere I turned, I was getting the Word straight out of the Book about sin being sin and how a person could miss receiving eternal life.

I was ready to do battle, but Elizabeth had changed her tactics. She was allowing me to read for myself. That night she admitted that she was attending the church during the week. She even tried to get me to go with her. This activity continued for five weeks. Every morning and night, I'd read the scriptures she'd marked for me and close the books. She must have bought two dozen copies, because I found them in my bathroom, on my bedside stand, beside every ashtray in the house and even in the refrigerator next to the milk.

In addition to all this, Elizabeth was continuing to change. She was becoming more loving. I was being loved in a way that I'd never experienced. She seemed to be becoming "holy" and I couldn't understand it. I was beginning to feel dirty beside her! I knew I had to do something to break the cycle of our lives. She was loving me so much that I was getting sick of being loved. In desperation, I made my move.

"Honey," I proposed one evening after dinner, "tonight let's go to a movie."

"You know I can't," she replied.

"Why can't you?" I demanded. "You're my wife and I want to go to a movie. We're not even acting like a man and wife. All we do together is read the Bible. Let's go out and have some fun."

A different sparkle entered her eyes. "Okay," she agreed. "I'll go to the movie with you if you'll come to church with me."

She knew if I promised her something, I'd keep my word, and when I said, "Okay, I'll go to church," she gave me the biggest smile I'd ever received. All four of us—my son Tommy Jr., my three-year-old daughter Shirley, Elizabeth and I went off to the movie. During the show, Elizabeth and Shirley spent 80 percent of their time in the ladies' restroom. This really didn't concern me, because I had little Tommy with me. I knew she was with me, and this meant that I'd have a chance to work on her, and if luck was with me, I could start changing her back into the kind of woman I could understand and control. When I married Elizabeth, I didn't want a saint, and that's what she was becoming.

That was on a Saturday night, and the next morning she

called on my promise. We were still in bed when she rolled over and whispered, "Daddy, you said you'd go to church with me. Let's get up and go."

I had no choice. I had to go. Had I known then what she was doing in that restroom all that time, I'd have felt relieved of my promise, but I didn't learn that until years later. While sitting in the movie, God had told Elizabeth that if He was coming for her, He wouldn't enter that theater. She'd spent all that time in the restroom praying for me! On Sunday morning, if I'd known about her prayers, I'd have blown my stack. She couldn't have gotten me into her stupid church, and I'd have walloped the daylights out of her for thinking she was good enough to pray for me. There'd been only one woman in my life good enough for that, and Elizabeth wasn't that woman.

According to Webster, pride means "an overhigh opinion of oneself; exaggerated self-esteem; conceit and haughty behavior resulting from this." This definition fit me to a tee. My pride was so great that I couldn't see beyond it. It was the justification for my sin. God knew exactly what I had to learn, and He proceeded to teach me. Both Christians and non-Christians alike find it extremely easy to confuse pride with dignity. Webster defines dignity as "the quality of being worthy of esteem or honor." In my mind, dignity and pride always meant the same thing.

If I had been the great Christian I considered myself to be, I'd have known how Jesus classified pride. In Mark 7:20-23, He includes pride with several other human attributes. "That which cometh out of the man, that defileth the man. For from within, out of the heart of men, proceed evil thoughts, adulteries, fornications, murders, thefts, covetousness, wickedness, deceit, lasciviousness, an evil eye, blasphemy, pride, foolishness: all these evil things come from within and defile the man."

Wearing my religious pride on my sleeve, I left the house that Sunday morning to go to church with Elizabeth. Neither of us said very much during the drive, but my brain was active. I was aware of a big change in her and I wasn't sure I could handle a whole church full of people like her. It just wasn't natural for people to be as happy and loving as she'd been during the weeks of our Bible exploration. After parking the car, she led me inside the building.

The sight that greeted me was unbelievable. There were about 170 people present and, counting the preacher, I was the tenth man. Everyone was hugging each other and everyone I met was happy to see me. Nothing like this ever happened at any of the Baptist churches I'd attended. The main interest I'd found in them was if my pledge was paid up or not. It rarely was, but I justified that by using my unpaid amount as a weapon to make them notice me.

Looking around the room, and seeing the unbalanced sexual composition of the congregation, I couldn't help thinking, "This can't be much of a church if only 10 men show up on a Sunday morning. We have almost as many deacons in my church as they have people here."

A couple of the men, when we were introduced, even tried to hug me. They got an elbow in their ribs for their effort. I wasn't going to have some religious nut pawing over me. I'd shake hands with any man, but it was damned unnatural for men to hug men! Elizabeth was hugging everyone, and I silently resolved to speak to her about being so free with her affections. I'd heard rumors about these full gospel people and what I was seeing certainly seemed to point toward the truth of those stories. In my mind, I knew this whole little church was a "hotbed of holy rollers." I was about to walk out in disgust, taking Elizabeth with me, when she sensed my intentions.

"You promised," she whispered, "and you've got to keep your promise!"

God must have laughed when He saw my unholy pride in the fact that my word was my bond keep me in that church for the complete service. And what a service it was! I immediately disliked the preacher. He was in charge of this peculiar crowd and I couldn't trust him.

Elizabeth led me to a pew just five rows back from the front. There was no way for me to leave during the service without attracting undue attention to myself. Some of the people sat in the choir and everyone else snuggled up together, and they started singing. I hadn't heard singing like that in a long time. It reminded me of the times my mother had taken me to church and I'd watch her raise her arms in the air and sing to the Lord. She'd get so involved in her singing that the hairpins in her hair would fly out and fall on me. Oh, we had good singing in my church, but it was nothing like this.

Looking around at the crowd, I couldn't understand how any group of people could be this happy on a Sunday morning. I knew they hadn't been drinking, and I wished that I had. They were crying and singing at the same time, but their tears weren't those of sadness. Some of them even had their arms raised while others were clapping their hands in time with the music. Without doubt, I thought, this whole crowd is crazy! The worst was still to come!

When the singing stopped, the pastor got up and prepared to preach. He was a short, fat man. His triple chin looked like rings of fat, and they jiggled wildly when he laughed, and he laughed about almost everything he said. He was a happy man and when he smiled or grinned, his large mouth revealed a gleaming, full set of false teeth. There was simply no way this man could be a true servant of God. In my opinion, he was unfit to serve himself, let alone the Lord my mother had worshiped.

The Reverend Mr. Anderson surveyed the crowd with a beaming, pockmarked face and called for testimonies. Several people got to their feet and praised God for saving them from alcohol, for putting their marriages back together, and one woman actually pointed at her husband and proclaimed, "God saved my man from a life of sin!" All I needed was for Elizabeth to do something like that.

I needed almost everything these people were claiming, but my pride wouldn't let me admit it. I needed my marriage saved. I was paying good money to the lawyer for that. I needed to be freed from alcohol. It was killing me by adding to my high blood pressure. I needed to be saved from sin, but I knew if it was going to be done, I'd have to do it. Asking God to help me was something I just couldn't do. I never heard anyone ask God for such help in my church with its 10,000 members. Not one of our 120 deacons ever suggested such a thing. My mindset was against it, and Reverend Anderson and his crowd of loonies weren't about to change it. I knew I was "saved," and that's all there was to it!

The testimony died down, and then some of them got up and requested prayers for healing. Anderson waved them up to the front and started praying. He anointed them with oil and called on God to give them new hearts, lungs, legs, eyes and whatever else they said they needed. This didn't bother me too much because Mother had also prayed for such things, but then God listened to her. She'd proved that when I was so ill.

All the time this was happening, Elizabeth's eyes never left my face. Her lips were silently moving, and I knew she was praying for me. My reaction, once again, was one of resentment. The healing prayers ended, and then Anderson started to preach.

He'd be going on about sin and damnation, looking across the room, but pointing directly at me! All five fat fingers on his right hand were aimed at my "innocent" head! He'd cut loose about the evils of smoking, gambling and drinking, and those fingers seemed to stab right into my eyes. I'd look up at his laughing face and hear him describing the terrors of hell and bear the full impact of his condemning fingers. Everything he said applied to me and the things I was doing, but he was laughing about it! According to him, I was going to hell, and it seemed to make him happy.

I didn't know what conviction was, but I was learning fast. As Anderson put it, the three times I'd been baptized meant nothing if I continued to sin. He didn't lay it on me with a delicate trowel, he was using a great big scoop shovel! It was obvious Elizabeth had told him everything about me. No man on earth could preach such a personal sermon without knowing the facts of my life. I could hardly wait to get her outside in the car!

Anderson made his "altar call," and I got to my feet and headed for the door. Once outside, I lit a cigarette and waited for Elizabeth. When she finally arrived, I laid it on her.

"Okay, now we've gone to all the other churches in town and we've gone to this one, and that's it. I'll have no more of what I saw and heard this morning."

"Why, Daddy?" she asked.

"Why?" I roared. "You told that preacher everything I was doing. He's blabbed it to all those people, and I'm never going back. Those people know things about me that they have no business knowing, and I'm not going back. Is that understood?"

Protest filled her beautiful face as she said, "Daddy, I didn't tell anyone anything about you."

"You had to," I shouted. "He couldn't know me that well. Anderson told me everything I've been doing, and then he told me that I was going to hell and he was happy about it! I don't like him and I don't want him around! I'm not going back, and that's that."

For the next five weeks, I heaped my resentment on her. I accused her of running around with other men. In the process, I became convinced that she didn't want me any more, that she wanted someone else. Every time I thought about Anderson and his church, my blood pressure would shoot up several notches. I'd resolved never to enter any church again, but God knew the strength of my resolutions and continued with His plan.

The face that now looked back at me in that aircraft restroom mirror wasn't the face I carried those long-ago days in Houston. My memories to this point had been bitter to recall. They seemed to crowd in on me in the small confines of the airborne room. I could hear the rush of wind just outside the thin skin of the plane, and it seemed to echo the voice in my heart which was saying, "It's all right, Tommy, I understand."

# Chapter 6
## MY WIFE'S OTHER LOVE

*"And Jesus looking upon them saith, 'With men it is impossible, but not with God: for with God all things are possible."*

Mark 10:27

Coming out of the restroom, I was confronted by an attractive woman seated alone in the darkened lounge. She was wearing a trim burnt-orange suit with a short skirt that just covered her knees. She smiled before she spoke.

"Mr. Ashcraft, if you're not too sleepy I'd appreciate a few minutes of your time."

We'd been in flight for about four hours and even though we were racing the clock toward the west, my two naps had forestalled the effects of jet lag. I sat down in the seat across from her and waited for her to continue.

Nodding her head toward the aircraft pantry, she said, "One of the flight attendants told me your name. I'm Ruth Madsen, and my husband is sound asleep back in our seats." She smiled again and seemed to study the hem of her skirt. "I hardly know how to begin, but the young lady," and again she nodded toward the pantry, "said that you could help me."

"Why don't you start at the beginning," I softly suggested.

"I don't think we have time for that," she answered, "but I'll try." Glancing toward the pantry, she asked, "Is it true that you were once an alcoholic?"

Getting up, I moved to the seat beside her. "I was an alcoholic," I admitted, "but God took away my need for liquor."

Her hands were shaking slightly as she took a cigarette from the package in her bag. Placing it in her lips, she unsuccessfully tried to strike her lighter. I took it from her hand, struck a flame and held it to the cigarette as I asked, "Do you have a drinking problem?" She put her lighter back in her open bag as I waited for the answer. It came with an exhaled cloud of smoke.

"Yes."

"Do you want to do something about it?"

"I have to," she admitted, "it's ruining my life."

"But do you want to?"

She glanced at me and then looked away as she said, "As God is my witness, I want to stop."

"Can you admit you're an alcoholic?"

Tears were streaming down her cheeks as she looked me straight in the eyes and nodded her head.

"Then say it," I gently pressed.

"I want a drink so badly right now that I'd do almost anything to get it. Is that alcoholic enough for you?"

"No," I said. "You're going to have to admit you're an alcoholic and claim the title before anyone can help you." Reaching out, I took her hand in mine and asked, "Did the flight attendants refuse to serve you a drink?"

"Yes."

"Why? You don't seem drunk to me."

"My husband's a doctor, and he asked them not to." She took a deep breath and then let her story come out in a desperate rush.

For almost a month, she and Dr. Madsen had been in England, where he was lecturing on the new surgical techniques he'd helped develop in human organ transplants at a Houston medical center. Ruth's constant drinking hadn't caused a serious problem until their last night in London, when Dr. Madsen was being honored at a banquet. While he was giving his farewell address, she had slipped out for a round of "pub crawling" on her own. That morning, the police had called him to come and get her from the Soho District Station.

"Yes, I'm an alcoholic," she finally admitted with a free flow of tears.

Gently squeezing her hand, I observed, "With that admission, you've just won half the battle. Now, you no longer have to fight the problem by yourself." We were both unaware that Dr. Madsen had entered the darkened lounge and was standing silently nearby.

"Who will help me?" she asked.

"The greatest Helper of them all," I answered. "You and I will pray and ask Jesus to heal you. We'll ask Him to come into your heart and be the Lord of your life." I took the dead cigarette from her shaking hand, and stubbed it into an ashtray. With both her hands in mine, I started to pray.

"Lord Jesus, Ruth and I are asking You to touch her with Your love and stop her hands from shaking." She was nodding her head in agreement when Dr. Madsen touched his wife's arm. "We ask You now to lift her desire and need for alcohol. We admit that You're the Lord of heaven and earth and through You all things are possible." Placing my right hand on the doctor's arm, I continued, "With their agreement, Lord, I ask that You enter their hearts and give them the blessings of the Holy Spirit so they can minister to each other in Your name." Both of their heads were nodding and a whispered "Yes" came from Ruth's lips. "We can all say 'Jesus is Lord,' and with that we pray in Your name. Amen."

All the strength left Ruth's body, and she settled deeper in her seat. A flash of concern crossed the doctor's face and he reached for her wrist. He looked at me with alarm in his eyes.

"She's resting in the Spirit," I explained. "She'll be all right. You can check her if you wish, but God is healing her right now, and when she rejoins us she'll be a new woman." Getting to my feet, I watched him check her pulse and smile with medical assurance. I motioned for him to sit beside her. "I'm Tom Ashcraft, and your wife asked for my help."

"I overheard most of your conversation," he said, "and I want to thank you for getting her to admit she's an alcoholic."

"Dr. Madsen, right now your wife is healed of that problem, but you're going to have to help her stay healed."

"How?"

"You've got to give her your love and support while she's fighting her battle. The Devil will tempt her, and she'll need your help to resist. Jesus wants her healed, but she can still turn away." He nodded his understanding and agreement as I added, "And I think you should change your lifestyle and friends."

Once again he asked, "How?"

"Do you attend a church?"

"We're Presbyterians, but we don't go very often."

"Then start going every Sunday. Get involved with other Christians. Tonight, you both asked Jesus into your hearts and with Him as the Lord of your lives, nothing will be impossible for you. I'm a member of the Full Gospel Business Men's Fellowship International, and I want both of you to attend our regular chapter meetings in Houston."

While I was explaining the Fellowship to him, Ruth rejoined us. Her hands were no longer shaking, and there was a joy in her eyes that hadn't been there before. Dr. Madsen observed the change and took her in his arms. They were still weeping with happiness when we jointly thanked God for His miracle and I returned to my seat.

"Where were the Christians who really knew the Lord when I needed them?" I asked myself.

The voice in my heart answered. "They found you, Tom, just as I did. Don't you remember?"

Adjusting my seat as far back as it would go, I closed my eyes and let my memory carry me back in time to the evening Elizabeth told of finding someone else to love more than she loved me. I'd been drinking and gambling with my friends at the bowling alley earlier that night and had just gotten into bed, when she dumped it on me. I could feel her breath on the back of my head as she spoke.

"Daddy, I have a confession to make."

I must have grunted or something to let her know I was still awake, but I really didn't want to hear any of her silly confessions. It might mean that I was supposed to confess something to her in return, and I had no intention of doing that! She was speaking very softly, but I heard every word.

"Up until now I've loved you more than anyone else on the face of the earth, but I've found someone else that I love more."

This got my attention, and I rolled over and faced her. In all this time, I'd never doubted her fidelity. Sure, she'd been the one to ask for the divorce, but I'd never suspected another man. I was hurt, but my pride wouldn't let me admit it. "Okay," I growled, "if that's what you want!"

"No, Daddy, you don't understand."

"What's to understand?" I retorted.

"But, Daddy," she implored, "the person I've found is Jesus. It's Him that I love more than you!"

This really hurt me, and I said, "How can you love someone more than me when you can't even see Him?" Anger began to rise in my breast. "You've lived with me for 10 years. I've put the food on your table and the roof over your head. I'm the father of your children." Jealousy poured in on me like salt into an open wound. I know now that I should have been a happy man, but I was still living in the flesh, and my reaction was from the flesh. "How can you possibly love Jesus more than me?" I demanded.

Pleading for understanding, she murmured, "Jesus has to come first in my life. It can't be any other way."

My smoldering pride burst into flame. "Okay, okay," I yelled while rolling away from her. "If that's the way you want it, then that's the way you're going to get it!"

Silence settled over our bedroom, but I didn't sleep. My thoughts, emotions and soul were in turmoil. I was hurt, angry and prideful. Elizabeth had forsaken me for a person I knew she could neither see nor feel. She was becoming a religious fanatic! The crazy people at that crazy church had turned her against me! They had succeeded in destroying her love for me! I was her husband, but she loved Jesus more than me. When I finally slept, my heart was filled with pain and a seed of hate was planted deep within me that would have to be torn out by the roots.

The passage of each succeeding day allowed my hatred and resentment to grow. I started staying out later each night and my drinking and gambling increased. The following Sunday morning when Elizabeth announced that she and the children were going to church, I announced that I was going to the bowling alley. Storming out of the house, I peeled rubber on our driveway as I sped away. By taking the car, I'd left her afoot, and I didn't think she'd walk to that church. She didn't; they came and picked her up.

By three-thirty in the afternoon, I was half drunk and I'd lost close to $400. It wasn't my day for cards and with some grumbling I left the game. Standing alone at the bar with a drink in hand, I debated going back home. My stomach rumbled from the lack of food, and I headed for the door. Satan took one more swipe at me as I thought, "Yeh, Elizabeth will be there loving Jesus and waiting to rub my nose in her new love!" My mood was dark and belligerent when I parked the car in the driveway.

Entering the house, I was greeted by the laughter and conversation of at least 20 happy people. The aroma of food cooking in the kitchen filled my senses. She'd invited a whole pack of fanatics to dinner. The living room was full of people talking about Jesus. The dining room was packed with widows, orphans and that fat preacher. I went straight to my bedroom, speaking only to the ones that spoke to me. Closing the bedroom door, I couldn't stop the sounds of their praises from reaching me. I locked myself in the bathroom, but I could still hear them. My stomach again rumbled with hunger, and I knew I'd have to join them if I wanted anything to eat. Using my mouthwash to cover my liquor breath, I straightened my tie, put on a brave face and headed for the kitchen. I'd let Elizabeth know that I was home and expected to be fed.

I got as far as the dining room. Elizabeth and several other ladies were putting food on the table. Reverend Anderson and his wife were standing beside her. He beamed at me and surveyed the room with nodded approval. They'd pushed tables together, and Elizabeth had used every dish in the house, but everyone was going to sit down at the same time for the meal. Indicating the chair at the head of the table by pulling it back, Anderson spoke loud enough for everyone in the house to hear.

"Mr. Ashcraft, we're so very happy that you returned in time to join us. Please take your rightful place here at the head of the table."

My anger almost flared out of control, but I jammed it back

down inside me. Who did he think he was, welcoming me to dine here in my own home? I knew that he'd intended sitting at the head of the table and was only stepping aside to save us having a fist-fight. His wife was smiling sweetly, and I hated her too. She considered herself to be half-preacher and really too good for the likes of me, but she'd tolerate me, because this was my home. Wishing I'd never left the bowling alley, I pressed my way through the people to my chair. They were all praising Jesus, and I'd had about all I could stand. Jesus was coming out of my ears. I was choking on Jesus. My blood pressure was building to new heights, and Jesus was stuck in my throat!

The food was on the table, and everyone had found a chair. Some idiot asked Anderson to bless the food, and I bowed my head. I'd show them that I knew how to be a Christian. I'd been raised in a God-fearing family. My father always blessed the food before we ate. I'd never done it, because I didn't know how to pray, but I'd been raised right and knew how to act when someone else prayed. The blessing my dad asked before each meal had always been short and to the point, but that wasn't Anderson's style. He started running off at the mouth, and I didn't think he'd ever stop.

Anderson prayed for a few minutes and then the people started singing. He prayed some more, and they sang some more. I was waiting for the "amen," and it never seemed to come. I was hungry, and the food was getting cold, but they just kept on praising Jesus. I'd never heard people pray like this. It seemed to go on for half an hour. I was about to jam the bowl of mashed potatoes in Anderson's face, when he suddenly sat down and started passing food. I don't remember anyone saying "amen," but right then I didn't care. They were at least beginning to eat!

I don't know how much that dinner cost me in money, but I

know my pride paid a terrible price. Somehow we got through the meal, and I found myself alone in the living room with Anderson. Everyone else was helping Elizabeth with the cleaning up, and I felt the need for a nap, but with the preacher at my elbow that was impossible. Resolving to punch him out if he just once mentioned Jesus, I sat down to talk.

As it turned out, the Reverend Anderson was a great hunter and fisherman. He knew all the best places to find fish and game. We swapped stories about the big fish we'd caught and those that had gotten away. Not once did he mention Jesus. I forgot about all the rest of the people. He even invited me to go fishing with him, and I happily accepted. I don't know how long we'd been visiting when he glanced at his watch and exploded.

"Great Scott!" he exclaimed. "Look at the time. I'm supposed to be at the church!"

We got up and called for the others, but we were alone. Looking outside, he saw his car was gone. The only car left was mine, and I knew before he asked me, that I was going to have to drive him to the church. I'd promised myself never to go back there, but now I had to take him. He wasn't such a bad guy after all, I decided. He loved to fish and hunt, and he could spend an afternoon talking as a friend without preaching about Jesus. I got my hat and coat, and we headed for the car.

Anderson was now my friend. We were going fishing together. When he invited me to stay for the service, I accepted. At least this time, I thought, he won't come down on me with everything he preached. Boy, was I wrong!

That man turned into a viper when he got behind the pulpit. He'd look the other way and point to me every time he zeroed in on a mighty hell-committing sin. He knew more about me than it was possible for any mortal to know. I was sitting between Elizabeth and my daughter, and they were holding my hands. I couldn't move without breaking away from them. I was trapped and just had to sit there and take it. Anderson had been so friendly, and now he was tearing me apart. Everything he laid his tongue to applied to me and his smiling face told me that he enjoyed putting me to the fire. I knew that if I ever got that man anywhere near a fishing stream, I'd drown him and laugh with glee as his life bubbled away.

He'd preach about the sin of drinking, and I'd get a great craving for a drink. He'd get going about fornication, and I'd think of the girls I'd known. He'd carry on about lying, and I couldn't look Elizabeth in the eyes. He'd go on about our bodies being the temples of God, and I'd taste the anguish of wanting a cigarette. He came down hard on the sin of gambling, and my thinner wallet burned in my hip pocket. He was burying me in a mountain of conviction.

After every onslaught, I'd take refuge in the fact that I belonged to the biggest church in Houston. His church only had 10 male members and mine claimed a membership of 10,000 souls. I'd been baptized three times in water and paid $10 every month to the glory of God. We had more people in the choir than he had in total membership. What did he know about God and sin? I was saved. All the elders in my church were saved, and I was as good a Christian as they were. Anderson was crazy, and I knew it! I tried tossing his sermon back to someone who needed it, but it stuck to my fingers. I couldn't shake it loose. I started to sweat and my heart was pounding wildly. A rush of heat came over me coupled with renewed anger. I didn't think he was ever going to stop condemning me, but at last he ran out of vile things to lay at my feet, and made his altar call.

"If anyone here tonight doesn't know Jesus, and he wants to experience His great love and His forgiveness for his sins, let him come forward now and we'll pray for him."

We all got to our feet, and four or five people started walking forward. Every place I looked, I saw happiness and joy. I wanted that happiness and joy, but I didn't know how to get it. Anderson was asking me to come forward and give my heart to Jesus. He wanted me to admit that I was a sinner in front of all the people and beg him to pray for me. I couldn't do that. My pride wouldn't let me. All my life I'd considered myself a little better than other people and, going up to that altar, I'd have to publicly admit that I was a sinner. Standing there with my little daughter in my arms, I listened to the people sing "Just As I Am, Without One Plea." When they started the second verse, I heard a small voice speak somewhere inside me.

"I want you to give Me your heart."

Everything in me said, "Go to the altar," but I couldn't. I looked at the altar, and it seemed a mile away. I simply couldn't move either foot! I was frozen with shock! I started shaking and gently lowered my daughter to the pew. My mouth was suddenly dry. I wanted to go to the altar, but another voice was speaking inside me.

"Tommy, you know you can't lead the life these people expect of you. You already belong to a church. If your church hasn't got it, how can you get it here?" That contrary voice seemed to grow in volume when it asked, "How about your employees? You know you have to curse them to get them to work. How about the 11 guys you gamble with? What are they going to think about you when you become too pure to play with them?"

Once again I heard the other voice say, "Tom, give Me your heart! Do it now!"

I felt a hand on my shoulder. It was one of the men who'd been at my house for dinner. He smiled and asked, "Would you like to go the altar and pray?"

That did it! He'd judged me, and I knew it! He'd eaten my food, and now he was calling me a sinner. I cut loose on him with everything I could lay my tongue to. Faces around me showed shock and disbelief. I concluded my tirade by saying, "You can go to the altar and pray if you want to, but leave me alone!" He turned away with pain in his eyes as I added, "I'll pray when I feel like I need it, not when you or someone else thinks I should."

Working my way toward the door, I could think of nothing but getting out of there. I couldn't walk up to the altar, because it was too far, but I covered twice the distance to reach the door because my pride gave me the strength.

Once outside, I reached in my breast pocket for a cigarette. Lighting it, I started down the church steps. Taking the first one in anger, I said to myself, "I'm never coming back here." On the second step, my resolve grew stronger. "There's not going to be any more church for me! I'm confused and I don't know how to get what they've got, and I don't need it!"

Standing on the next step, I loudly proclaimed, "I'm through with all of this!"

I took a deep drag on my cigarette and stepped down to the fourth and last step. With one foot on the ground, I heard a loud, forceful voice.

"You make one more step and it's your last chance!"

I froze in that position and looked around for the source of that voice. I was alone! There was no one outside except me.

"One more step, Tom Ashcraft, and I'm through with you!"

That voice rang in my ears, and I knew it was God speaking from heaven.

# Chapter 7
# ONE SECOND FROM HELL

*"But new wine must be put in new bottles; and both are preserved."*

**Luke 5:38**

My heart was pounding with excitement, and the echo of that heavenly voice was ringing in my ears. I knew I was at a critical crossroad in my life, but my knowledge of God was limited. I didn't know what He expected of me.

"Lord, what must I do?"

The beating of my heart was the only sound I could hear. No further instructions were issued by the voice in my heart. I was alone. There was no one else to turn to. If I took one more step into the secular world, I knew God would turn His back on me, and a deep fear began to swell in my breast. I don't remember going back up those church steps or re-entering the building. Somehow I accomplished that long walk to the altar rail and faced Pastor Anderson, the man whom I'd hated so strongly just a few minutes before. My blood pressure was at its peak. My mouth was dry, and I could hardly speak. Anderson's eyes locked on mine and his voice sounded as if he were a thousand miles away.

"Brother Ashcraft, what's troubling you?"

The singing had stopped. The entire church was silent. I could almost feel the silence gathering around me. God was there, and I could sense the expectations of the people. For the first time in my life, I understood the meaning and purpose of fearing God. Suddenly, I knew that He was the Master of everything and everyone. In that same instant I knew that my pride had made me a servant of Satan. My judgment day was at hand! I felt as if I were having a heart attack! The pressure inside me was about to explode!

"Help me," I breathlessly pleaded. "Someone help me!"

The voice I'd heard on the front steps had filled me with terror. The true understanding of hell had been born in my heart. I was a sinner, and I felt as if I were dying. I knew that God could take my life at any time, and I wasn't ready. If I died right then, I knew I'd burn forever! "I'll do anything," I screamed, "but somebody has to help me!"

I'd never given my heart to God or Jesus. In my mind, I knew about God, but it had never been a matter of personal concern for me. I'd taken refuge in my church membership, never thinking that God could or would demand more. I hadn't even completely given my heart to Elizabeth. My selfishness with love had always been viewed from the receiving angle, not the giving. The closest I'd ever come to giving love was to my mother, and even then, I'd done it with a selfish interest. She had been my prayer power, and by loving her, I'd gotten as close to God as I thought I needed to be.

The murmur of whispered prayers seemed to rise in the air around me. All those loving people whom I'd resented so strongly just a few moments before were praying for me. The real truth then hit me. I knew I was the only one who could really help me. I knew that God wanted me to surrender my heart to Him. Pastor Anderson confirmed this new knowledge.

"Tom," he said, "you're the only one who can do anything about your troubles. Kneel down, right where you're standing," he commanded, "and tell God you're a sinner! Tell Him that you've sinned in thought, word and deed! Tell Him you're sorry and beg His forgiveness! Tell Him that you'll accept Jesus as your Savior and make Him the Lord of your life!"

All the scriptures that Elizabeth had left open for me to read flashed through my mind. Romans 10:9-10 came down on me with new power and meaning. I knew I had to confess my sins! I finally understood the divine value of forgiveness. I reached for it with my whole heart. Every evil and selfish thing I'd done in my life crowded in on me. Knowing that I couldn't recall them all, I got on my knees and begged God to remember them and forgive me. It made no difference that everyone was hearing what a low-down sinner I'd been. At that moment, I was talking to God and that's all that mattered. He was hearing me and my burden was becoming lighter. I was opening my heart to Jesus! Right in the middle of all this, another voice spoke within me.

"You're being silly, Tommy. This isn't for you. You've committed too many sins to be forgiven. Why should Jesus forgive you? What have you ever done for Him?"

It was the voice of my old master! Satan was talking to me! He was trying to turn me away from salvation! I'd lived with the Devil so long that I thought his ideas were my own. The Devil tried to make me aware of what I was saying, of the evil things I'd done and was now confessing for anyone to hear. He was trying to make my pride keep me in bondage to sin. I turned him off by proclaiming, "Jesus is Lord!"

The words Elizabeth had left for me to read came roaring into my feverish brain. "But if we walk in the light, as He is in the light, we have fellowship one with another, and the blood of Jesus Christ His Son cleanseth us from all sin." These words told me that I could be forgiven. They were my assurance that I could be saved.

Having never really spoken to God, I found it extremely hard to call on Him, but I finally got it out. "God," I said, "I'm a

terrible sinner." Once I'd actually given voice to my sins, I
started crying. Up until that moment all my tears had been for
pain, as a child, and grief, as an adult. The last time I'd shed
tears had been at the death of my mother, but now my tears
were flowing with relief and joy.

I didn't understand it then, but I was dying to the flesh and
being born again in the Spirit. The shackles on my heart were
being broken, and a new peace was being created in my soul.
When I acknowledged Jesus as my Savior, my blood pressure
dropped. Through my confession, God had turned my stone-
cold heart into a warm, living thing. "Jesus is my Savior," I
declared, "and I promise to live my life for Him." I meant every
word that I said and that's promising it with your heart and
confessing Him with the lips, and with that simple declaration,
and the forgiveness of God, I became the adopted brother of
Jesus and a child of God.

Tears still streaming from my swollen eyes, I looked up at
Pastor Anderson and saw that he also was weeping. His joy in
my salvation was the first act of brotherly love that God was
giving me. Anderson no longer seemed ugly, and all traces of
my former hatred were gone. He was a beautiful man, and I
loved him. A new sense of total peace engulfed me. My desire
for booze was gone. My heart was filling with love. Jesus also
lifted my need to gamble and the package of cigarettes in my
shirt pocket became a useless burden. Realization that all this
was taking place within me began seeping into my brain.

With a living stream of love flowing into me, I had to give it
away. I thought my heart would burst and turned to face the
people. The man who'd felt the sharpness of my elbows when
he tried to embrace me was standing nearby. I hugged that man
with a new spirit of love. The women that I'd shied away from
before were suddenly my dearly beloved sisters. Looking at my

wife and children, I was overwhelmed by a new sensation of tenderness. I'd loved Elizabeth sexually, but this was different. She was no longer an object for my pleasure. Her beauty had multiplied in my mind, and I pushed through the people to the pew where she was standing.

Putting my hands on her shoulders, I held her weeping eyes with mine. There was something I had to do before I could embrace her with my new love. "Darling, I hardly know how to say this, but I have to tell you how deeply sorry I am for all the nasty and hurtful things I've done. Please forgive me." She nodded her sweet head and reached out for me.

We were locked in each other's arms, and I could feel the arms of my son and daughter hugging us from the sides. For the first time in our marriage, we were truly a family. I half-sobbed in her ear, "I promise you with all my heart that I'll never do anything to hurt you again."

Elizabeth protested, "But, Daddy, it wasn't all your fault."

Jesus and I both knew where the fault could rest, and it was squarely on my shoulders, but with her forgiveness that was no longer a matter for concern by either of us. My past wickedness had been given to Him, and it was no longer a matter of concern for God or any man.

We stood there in a sea of happiness. Elizabeth had experienced this new sense of freedom and love weeks before, and now we were sharing it. Everyone in that church had been praying for me and rejoicing with us. I was kissing men and women and being kissed without the slightest feeling of embarrassment. I was part of the family of God. I was a living stone in His Church. This was *agape* love. There was no sense of carnal shame in any of it. We were united in Christ.

My nine-year-old son and three-year-old daughter must have known that I'd changed. Their attitudes toward me began to turn from dutiful to loving. Up to that evening, they'd viewed me as a stern father, but the new softness I felt for Elizabeth was also for them.

Thinking back on that evening now, I can clearly see the vital difference in my salvation experience from anything I'd ever felt before in any church. I no longer had any doubt about the reality of heaven and hell. I was positive that God had claimed me and that if I died, I would go to heaven. Not one of the three water baptisms had given me this assurance. This isn't to say that members of those churches weren't saved. I know there are many members of those congregations who have a personal knowledge and relationship with God. My mother was one of them. She had made the necessary commitment to Jesus. She'd given Him her heart and life. In truth, I'd simply made this commitment for the first time. It could have happened in my old church, but it took the dedication of my dear brothers and sisters to get me over the hurdle of my pride. This loving concern for me is what I hadn't found in the biggest church in Houston.

Today, when I ask someone if he's saved, and he answers, "I think so," then I know he isn't. When a person is truly saved, he or she has absolutely no doubt about it. If he answers my question by saying, "I go to church every Sunday," then I know he hasn't made the salvation commitment. I know that Jesus isn't the Lord of his life and deep in his heart he's reserving something he doesn't want to surrender to Him.

This isn't to say that I no longer sin. I'm a sinner, but Jesus continues to forgive me and cleanse me of my sins when I give them to Him. I still feel the pull of lust and the thrill of taking a gamble, but they are no longer a burden to me, because I can give them to Him. My heart beats now with the assurance that God loves me, and all doubt has been removed. This is what

Jesus meant when He said, "For God so loved the world, that
He gave His only begotten Son, that whosoever believeth in
Him should not perish, but have everlasting life."

Being able to say, "I'm a born again Christian," means a great
deal more than we can at first assume. Jesus put it this way:
"Verily, verily, I say unto thee, except a man be born again, he
cannot see the kingdom of God." Being water-baptized isn't
enough. It isn't the complete born-again experience. Jesus
defined it for us: "Verily, verily, I say unto thee, except a man
be born of water and of the Spirit, he cannot enter into the
kingdom of God."

All of this wasn't entirely clear to me when I left the church
that Sunday night, but God was being patient with me and had
given all He knew I could digest at that point in my new
spiritual walk.

The following Monday morning, I saw in the faces of my
bakery subordinates the confirmation of the change in me.
Where I would usually greet them with a growl and a harsh
demand for greater effort; that morning I practically sang,
"Good morning. Did you have a nice weekend?" The startled
shock on their faces told me that I had changed. My
superintendents actually came to their office doors and watched
me with amazement as I went down the hallway toward my
office. They had absolutely no hint of what had happened to
me, and the wonder of it was almost too much for them. I'd
been a terrible man to work for, and my changed attitude made
them suspicious.

When lunch time came and I went out as usual, but returned
completely sober, I really think they began to doubt the state of
my health. Jesus had also cleaned up my language, and my
secretary was amazed by the lack of cursing over the phone and
in my general conversation. Once again, the Devil tried to

tempt me.

"Tommy, you're crazy if you think these people will do their jobs without being driven with hatred and vile language. Just wait and you'll see what all this Christian foolishness will do to the profits of your baking division."

"Get away from me," I firmly told him. "You're not the Lord of my life. Jesus has given me full power over you and in His name I command you to leave." I can't describe the actual joy I received from knowing that I no longer had to serve the master of hell. I'd never felt such freedom before, and it was like breathing clean air with clean lungs for the first time.

With my personal attitude changed so dramatically, the next two weeks became a delightful adventure. My gambling buddies simply couldn't understand what had happened to me. The bartenders at my old haunts were totally nonplussed by my going on the wagon. The ashtrays in my office were always empty, and my continued cheerfulness with my employees caused almost endless water-cooler gossip. None of them was truly aware of how much I'd changed. In fact, at that point I wasn't fully aware of what had taken place.

One of my greatest discoveries was how much the Bible had changed. It was as if I were reading a new book! Every verse contained a new meaning for me! Chapters that I'd read before were now different. I was perceiving new and profound meanings from everything I read in God's Word. It was as if God were talking directly to me. The letter Paul wrote to the Romans was now suddenly addressed to me. My mind was opening to new and startling understanding. While reading Luke 5, verses 37-39, I learned what was happening in my life.

"And no man putteth new wine into old bottles; else the new wine will burst the bottles, and be spilled, and the bottles shall perish. But new wine must be put into new bottles; and both are preserved. No man also having drunk old wine straightway desireth new: for he saith, the old is better."

The love and joy of my new relationship with Jesus couldn't be contained in the old lifestyle I'd been living. My body and its activities had to be changed to accommodate the life Jesus wanted me to live. I had to become a new bottle for the new wine of my spirit. My thinking had to change. The old values that had dictated my carnal life had to go. I had to accommodate a whole new set of priorities. I was no longer number one. Jesus was more important than I. I suddenly understood what Elizabeth had meant when she said, "I've found Someone I must love more than you."

For a moment, I resented this new understanding. During the days just past, I'd discovered a new and powerful love for my wife, and I didn't want to place her second to anyone. She had been second to so many things in my life, and it was as if God were now telling me to make her second again. It didn't make sense, and I was on the verge of rebellion, but the voice in my heart solved my dilemma.

"Tommy, give your love to Me, and I will return it a thousandfold. You must love the Lord your God with all your heart, mind and soul; and you must love your neighbor as yourself. Do this and you shall love Elizabeth as you've never loved her before!"

Right there in my office, I got on my knees and thanked God for the patience He'd shown with my stupidity. I had tried to rank my love for Elizabeth in the order of my old priorities, and God had gently shown me my error. The full meaning of Jesus' words as recorded by Luke hit me with fresh impact: "No man also having drunk old wine straightway desireth new: for he saith, the old is better." In those few minutes I'd learned a great truth.

With Jesus in my heart and the Lord of my life, I would be able to love my wife with greater depth and understanding than would ever be possible without Him. With this revelation also came the knowledge that I had a great deal of spiritual growing to do. I was still a babe in the Lord and had a long way to go before I'd become a man of God.

In the dim aircraft cabin light, I watched Helen, the South African hostess, fluff the pillow of a passenger three seats ahead of me. She glanced my way, and I raised my hand. Her brilliant white smile was like a beacon in the dark beauty of her face. Checking the sleeping passengers, she walked toward me. Leaning over my empty aisle seat, she whispered, "Can I get you anything, Mr. Ashcraft?"

"Do you still have some coffee?" I asked.

"I'm making a fresh pot for the flight deck. I'll bring you a cup."

I watched her briskly walk back to the forward galley and marveled at how much she and her companions seemed at home while flying 38,000 feet in the air. Their lives, I thought, must be composed of constant change and confusion, but they seemed to thrive on it. Betty and Shirley were nowhere in sight, and I assumed they had left Helen with the slower night duties and were taking a nap. The girls worked as a team, and Helen would get a break later in the flight.

After serving the flight deck, Helen returned with a tray containing two cups. It was obvious that she didn't intend for me to drink alone. Her warm soft voice confirmed her intentions.

"Do you mind if I join you?"

I lowered the service table from the back of the seat ahead of me and accepted the loaded tray while saying, "It would be my pleasure to have your company."

We were settled and had taken the first sips of our coffee when Helen kicked off her pumps and pulled her legs up under her in the seat. She looked cozy sitting half-sideways facing me. I couldn't help thinking how her friendly actions would have stimulated me 30 years earlier.

"Mr. Ashcraft," she asked, "can I talk to you about some very personal matters?" Without waiting for my reply, she continued. "I promise not to embarrass you, but I need some sound mature advice."

"If it's going to be that personal, Helen, I want you to call me Tommy."

She smiled and said, "If you don't mind, I'd prefer calling you Thomas. That was one of my father's names."

I nodded my approval.

After sipping her coffee, she closed her eyes and plunged into a rather startling confession. "Thomas, I've been living with a man for almost two years. We're deeply in love, but he's a third-year student at Rice University and doesn't want to get married until he's graduated." She opened her eyes and looked me directly in the face. "I feel that we're already married in the eyes of God, but what you said earlier about all of us serving a master makes me question if what we're doing is right. Society doesn't condemn us for living together, but I'm not sure about God."

"Have you ever discussed this with your young man?" I asked.

She nodded and sipped her coffee.

"What did he say?"

"He cited several examples of famous people who are living together and said, 'If it's good enough for them, why should we question it?' Up until now, I've accepted that, and we've lived accordingly." She smiled and murmured, "But then, neither of us has ever really thought about God and what He might think of what we're doing."

Reaching out, I touched her hand. "Helen, the fact that you're wondering about it now should prove that it's wrong."

"But until Harry graduates, he can't support me, and he refuses to accept the idea that I could go on working."

"How often are you together?"

"Not as much as we'd like," she sighed. "We'll have three days together on this layover, and then I'm off to London, Paris, Rome and Alexandria before I'll return. We spend about six days each month together."

"Helen, I can understand a man not wanting his wife hopping all over the world, but what you're doing is a sin, and you can burn in hell for it. Being married now wouldn't be perfect, but at least you wouldn't be committing adultery. Jesus will forgive your past sins, but He expects you to change and sin no more. If you will turn your relationship with Harry over to the Lord, He'll give you the answer you're seeking."

"You make it sound so simple, but I don't know how." She shook her head and added, "And I'm sure Harry wouldn't agree!"

"Are you sure Harry wants to marry you?"

"He says he does," she answered.

"Is he a Christian?"

"He's from Nigeria, and he attended the mission school in Horin. His mother and father were both Christians, but he's not a regular church-goer."

"If he's a Christian," I proposed, "then he'll agree to follow the guidance of our Lord. You belong to the Church of England, and Harry knows it. If he truly loves you, then he'll have to consider your feelings in this."

Helen finished her coffee as I finished mine, and she felt for her shoes with her feet. Bending forward, she got one on and turned her head toward me while fitting the other. "How can I give this problem to Jesus?" she asked.

"By asking Him into your heart and making Him the Lord of your life," I replied. "If you'd like me to pray with you, I will."

She whispered, "Please."

I led her in the sinner's prayer, and she asked God to forgive all her past sins. Everyone was asleep around us when she asked Jesus into her heart, and, at my suggestion, Helen asked for the baptism of the Holy Spirit. Jesus smiled on her and honored our prayer. Leaning back in her seat, she sat silently for several minutes, and then I dimly saw her smile. She patted my hand and softly said, "Jesus is Lord, and I praise Him for His great mercy. Thank You, Lord, for giving me the answer." Helen then started softly praying in a language I couldn't understand, and I knew she was talking to the Father of us all.

Fifteen minutes later, Betty found us, and her eyes filled with joy when she heard her companion's prayer. We both knew what had happened, and our hearts were full of love for Helen. She had met Jesus, and He was now living in her heart. When Helen looked up at Betty, she said, "Harry and I are going to be married. I want you and Shirley to be my bridesmaids." Before getting to her feet, she leaned over and kissed my cheek and asked, "Will you and Mrs. Ashcraft come to my wedding?"

I accepted and dabbed at the tears streaming from my eyes. The peace of God passes all understanding, but I'm constantly amazed at the swiftness with which He sets us straight when we surrender and ask. The two girls walked back to the galley arm in arm, and the voice in my heart said, "Thomas, I am truly pleased with you."

"It's Your glory, Lord," I confessed. "You found her, not I, and it's Your will that will be done on earth as it is in heaven."

"Yes," He answered, "just as I found you and you serve Me, Helen is now my beloved servant, and she will lead Harry back into the family of God."

Knowing Helen would still be tested by Satan, I prayed for her and asked Jesus to be with her as He was with me when my new faith was tested.

# Chapter 8
# GROWTH SITUATION

*"That your faith should not stand in the wisdom of men, but in the power of God."*

**I Corinthians 2:5**

Each of us, when we receive the baptism of the Spirit, undergoes a test of our newborn faith. For some this test comes right away, while others may wait months and even years before Satan hits them. It should also be added that our testing can continue over great periods of time. In fact, those of us walking in the Spirit with Jesus are in many ways under constant attack by the master of hell. Satan is the great deceiver, and without a fully matured gift of discernment, babes in Christ will often attribute thoughts and words from him as being from God. This in turn can lead us away from Jesus and back into bondage. I knew that Helen would be faced with this type of test and prayed that she'd find the Christian fellowship she'd need to survive.

I've known people, good people, who become so cocksure of their faith in their walk with our Lord that they become Spiritual Experts. When this happens, they become spiritually proud and want everyone to know that they have all the answers. I've seen this happen to ministers and priests, pastors and laymen, and I've watched them become bitter and judgmental in their relationships with those around them. Spiritual pride is a great sin, and Satan revels in the slime of its corruption. In his first letter to the Corinthians, Paul warned us about this very thing. The first four chapters of that holy book of the Bible are the inspired words of God and should be mandatory reading by every ministering and thinking Christian.

As a babe in Christ, I was totally unaware of all of this. To me, everything was new and shining. I had Jesus in my heart, and that was all I needed. The vestiges of my former pride were still present in my life, but I was blind to see it. I didn't understand that my new relationship with God would have to grow and change. I didn't realize that God expected more from me than simply being a good man. I wanted to serve Him, but I wanted to do it on my terms. After all, I'd quit drinking, gambling, smoking, chasing women and lying; what more could God ask? I was so pure and holy that my old gambling friends considered me odd. My employees could accept the new Tommy, but they were waiting for me to drop the other shoe.

God honored me with an immediate ministry. He allowed me to teach Sunday school in our new Pentecostal church. I'd never been able to sing in any fashion, except for an occasional drinking song, but all at once I found myself the music minister for the church. I was becoming a pillar of faith! I'd see friends from my old church and look on them as second-class Christians. I even got to the point where I asked God, "Why do I have to tell people that I'm a Christian? Why can't they see it?" I wanted to be humble, but I wanted people to know what a perfect Christian I'd become. I wanted people to understand what had happened to me, but I didn't want to tell them. In truth, I didn't want to brag about myself; I wanted them to do it for me!

Elizabeth and I would spend hours, sometimes until three or four o'clock in the mornings, studying scripture. We were both starved for God's Word and couldn't get enough of it. The bottle of Scotch that I kept in my desk at the office was replaced by a Bible. We had Bibles everywhere in the house. I carried one in the car, and whenever I had to wait for traffic or an appointment, I'd spend the time in the Word. Sure, I was making up for lost time, but there was another factor involved. I could understand scripture now, and I found it very exciting. Every day, Elizabeth and I would marvel over new meaning we'd found in the holy Word. We'd wonder if other people really knew the Truth as we were learning it.

I'd see secular books in people's homes or offices and wonder why they were wasting their time reading such trash when the Bible was all they needed. And with all this reading and studying, we still didn't understand that God intended using us as He saw fit. Not once did we think that we were preparing ourselves for a ministry that would not be of our choosing. I for one thought I had it made and was content to leave it that way. God had other plans, and part of my testing was still to come. Since that time, I've learned that every Christian has a ministry, and now I'll relate the story of how the voice in my heart led me to mine.

For three months—I call it my honeymoon with Jesus—everything went fine. My Sunday school classes were rolling along, and I was surprising myself as our music minister. Elizabeth and I had reconciled our marriage and were growing in the Spirit together. I no longer came home at odd hours and got the neighbors out of bed. There was an excitement in our lives that was joyous and pure. At this point, God gave me a brief taste of what He expected from me. It was almost as if He were trying me out to see how I'd react to a spiritual challenge.

The Hinke-Pillott Bakery, located on Washington Street in Houston, was a two-story building which contained our executive offices, a grocery store, drug store and cafeteria. I'd taken my lunch break and was standing in the cafeteria line when I noticed a man sitting at one of the tables. He looked to be about 55 years old and was wearing a dark suit and black hat. He wasn't a large man and he must have felt my gaze, because he looked up and caught my eyes. His eyeballs looked as if they were floating in oil, and he'd either been crying or was about to. "Oh, man," I said to myself, "that guy sure looks sick."

It was obvious he needed help of some kind, but I didn't think any more about it. God did a strange thing, however, and instead of selecting a lunch for myself, I simply got a cup of coffee and stood at the counter and drank it. All this while, I could feel the man's eyes on the back of my head.

When I'd finished my coffee, I walked outside to the parking lot. Standing there on the sidewalk, I felt a hand touch my shoulder. It was the same man. Up close, he looked even worse.

"Mister, would you pray for me?" he asked.

I'd never seen this man before in my life. I couldn't think of any possible way he could have known about me. Looking him up and down, I could almost feel his soul reaching out for help. Nothing like this had ever happened to me. Suddenly I thought of how I might have reacted in my drinking days and answered, "Sure, I'll pray for you. Where's your car?"

Pointing at the car right in front of us, he said, "This is it."

Stepping over to the passenger side, I suggested, "Let's get in, and I'll pray."

Once inside, he pulled off his hat and held it on the top of the steering wheel. He began telling me what was wrong, but all God allowed me to hear was that he needed Jesus. I was a new Christian, and I'd prayed for folks at the altar in church, but this was very different. I'd even made a couple of witnessing visits to the jail and handed out a few tracts on the street, but sitting with a stranger in a car listening to him pour his heart out was totally new. I held up my hand and stopped his confession.

"Don't tell me anything," I said. "I just want to pray for you. I want to pray that God will save you. That's what He did for me, and that's what He'll do for you."

Having said that, I began to pray. I had my eyes closed, but I could feel the presence of God in that car, and I could feel the stranger's submission. I led him in saying the sinner's prayer and then opened my eyes. He was weeping. Tears were streaming from his painful-looking eyes and soaking his hat. Knowing I was looking at him, he half-blubbered, "I'm sorry I'm such a sissy."

"That's all right," I conceded, "but do you believe that God has saved you?"

"Yes, I do, but," he held his fingers up as if measuring a short shot of whiskey and asked, "could we have one more little one?"

Nodding my head, I grabbed his hands and prayed, "God, I want You to solve this man's problems just like You solved mine. You've put my home together, forgiven me of all my sins, and I want You to do the same for my dear brother."

Nothing more was said. I got out of the car. We didn't shake hands or introduce ourselves to each other or anything. Walking around to the driver's side, I spoke to him through the open car window.

"I want you to come to my church." After telling him where it was, I amended, "If you don't want to come there, then get yourself a Bible and go to your own church. Go wherever you want to, but serve God from now on!" I watched him start his car and back away from the sidewalk. I didn't think I'd ever see him again, but I knew God had sent him to me.

A couple of months later, I spotted this same man walking

across the parking lot, not 100 feet from the spot where I'd prayed for him. He saw me and headed my way. The pain was gone from his face, and the tone of voice was entirely different.

"Mister," he called out as he approached, "you'll never know what you did for me."

"Don't thank me," I said. "Thank the Lord."

He nodded his head and continued to walk right past me.

Three more months passed, and once again I spotted him in almost the same place. I was headed for my car and when he saw me his arm shot up in the air as he yelled, "Mister, you'll never know what you did for me."

I called back, "Don't thank me. Thank the Lord!"

It was an additional three months before I saw him again and this time we just waved to each other. Almost a year after we'd prayed together, I was sitting in my office when my secretary announced a visitor. She explained that he wouldn't give his name and only wanted about 15 minutes. I told her to show him in.

It was my man, dressed in almost the same manner as the day I'd first seen him. He was smiling as he walked in and I asked him to sit down. He'd changed, and I thought at last I was going to hear about it. He introduced himself and I finally knew his name.

"Mr. Ashcraft," he said, "do you remember the day that I was sitting in the cafeteria and you spotted me?"

I nodded my reply.

"I want you to know," he continued, "that God told me you were the man to pray for me. All the time I was sitting there and you were drinking your coffee, God was telling me that you were my man. When I followed you outside and tapped you on the shoulder, God once again said, 'This is the man to pray for you.' I asked, and when you agreed, I knew it was God I was hearing."

I silently nodded.

"You see, Mr. Ashcraft, I'd never been to church in my life. I didn't know what a deacon was or anything else about religion. All the voices I'd ever heard were those that came to me in one of my drunken stupors." He studied his feet for a moment and then went on. "I had so much trouble that day, but when you prayed for me, God did save me!"

I started to speak, but remained silent.

"Then," he added, "when you asked God to solve all my troubles, you really laid it on the line for me. When I'd left home that morning, my wife had thrown me out. She'd told me that she never wanted to see me again. I was going with this other woman and she was threatening to kill me if I didn't leave my wife and marry her. Both of my children sided with their mother, and I was completely out."

He got up from his chair and walked to my office window before continuing. "When I arrived at work that morning, my boss fired me!" He turned and faced me. "At that moment, Mr. Ashcraft, life to me wasn't worth living. I came to your drugstore downstairs and bought some poison. I'd just gotten a glass of water and was preparing to add the poison. With the glass in one hand, the poison in the other, I looked up and saw you. That's when God said, 'That man will pray for you.' I had never thought of prayer, God or hell in my life, but that voice from out of nowhere made me put the poison in my pocket instead of the glass."

It briefly flashed through my brain that our company president would have been very upset if someone had died of poison in our cafeteria, but my friend's voice brought me back to reality.

"When you asked God to solve my problems, I decided to

take you at your word. With that prayer, you gave me hope. I
knew I had to resolve my problem with the other woman first,
and I went to her home. I told her if she wanted to kill me it was
okay. I figured that I was saved, and it didn't matter any more.
She hadn't even let me in the house and I figured she would
explode, but God had gotten there ahead of me. Speaking
through the screen door, she told me, 'John, I think it would be
better if you forgot about me and went back to your wife!' I
didn't hang around to argue the point."

I was silently praising Jesus for what I was hearing. John was
telling me how our Lord could take an impossible situation and
turn it completely around.

"When I went home," he continued, "and told my wife all of
that was behind me and begged her forgiveness, she welcomed
me back with open arms."

I could restrain myself no longer and shouted, "Hallelujah!"

John smiled and nodded his head, saying, "Yes, Mr.
Ashcraft, she forgave me, but God heard your prayer, and He
still had things for me to do. The very next day, I went down to
McKesson & Robbins and applied for a job. I got it," he
shouted, "at $25 a week more than I'd been making!" Leaning
toward me, he happily confided, "Not only that, but all traces
of my former heart trouble have vanished!"

I've related this story to demonstrate the wisdom of God.
Had He let me know and understand the extent of His miracle
just a few days after our brief prayer, I'd have gone wild. When
the Lord knew I was mature enough to see the results of His
power, without its destroying me as a tool, He sent John back
with his story. Jesus tested my willingness to serve Him without
allowing me to see the direct results. When I continued to
minister as He planned, without knowing what had happened,
He let me learn the truth.

All too often, when it seems our prayers are never answered, we cease to pray. This is an indication of the weakness of our faith. It's an indication of how immature we are in our walk with the Holy Spirit. Jesus knew how much I'd revered my mother's prayer power, and the premature knowledge that I, too, possessed it would have led me into the sin of spiritual pride. Satan would have had a heyday with me then, so I had to grow a year before I could be trusted with the knowledge. This wasn't the end of my testing, however, and I've come to understand that our testing really never ends. I believe that every step of our spiritual growth is tested and there's no limit to the growth we can experience.

Perhaps this is where each of my three water baptisms failed. The churches I attended never told me that I had more growing to do. They said I was saved and that's all there was to it. Whenever I'd begin feeling unsaved, back in the water I'd go and have my personal contract with God renewed. I can't remember ever being told that I could ask Jesus for anything more. Being saved was the ultimate victory, but now I understand what Jesus meant in His Sermon on the Mount when he said, "Therefore, be ye perfect, as your Father in heaven is perfect."

I know I'm not perfect to that divine degree. I still have a great deal of growing to do. That's why I say there's no limit to the growth we can achieve. That's why my testing will never end. Our Father in heaven tests us just as we test our children while they are growing. When we stop growing, He stops testing us. When we allow head-knowledge, the wisdom of men, to rule our lives the power of God ceases to be a factor in our growth. That's why spiritual pride is such a great sin. It can stand between us and the spiritual maturity and power that God wants us to have.

I wasn't aware of all this when John left my office that day. I was still a babe in Jesus, but I'd passed my first test. John was the first man I'd led to the Lord and when the miracle of his life was finally revealed to me, I understood how little I'd been involved in his victory. Jesus had saved him, not me. I had supported John with prayer, but the miracle was from Jesus.

John had been prepared to commit suicide. Satan had led him to the very bottom of his life. All that he'd achieved was worthless and life wasn't worth living. His head-knowledge had told him there was only one way out. How many people have been, or will be, led to this desperate level of existence without knowing they don't have to die! Satan isn't about to tell them, and that's why God wants us to be available with the witness of our salvation. The Lord understands that those who don't believe in Him or Satan may listen to another man. When I asked Jesus to save John's marriage the way He'd saved mine, I gave witness to an unbeliever of the power of God. That short witness gave John hope, and Jesus, in the love He has for all of us, did the rest. John submitted himself to the will of God with the hope my witness had given him. Paul says it so beautifully in his letter to the Romans: "For to be carnally minded is death, but to be spiritually minded is life and peace."

Sitting there in my seat, 38,000 feet over the Atlantic Ocean, I felt tears of joy filling my eyes. In recalling my life to me, Jesus was revealing the pattern of my own spiritual growth to me for the first time. He was allowing me to see how each test had made me stronger in my faith. Wiping my eyes, I leaned back in His arms and continued my reverie.

The year following my experience with John was filled with minor victories. I'd improved so much in my Sunday school teaching that I'd graduated to the high school youngsters. I was taking the Word of God to prison farms and giving witness of my salvation to anyone who'd listen. Elizabeth and I were happy and our family was growing. My work was going well and everything seemed in order, but one Sunday night I was brought face to face with the next step in my spiritual walk with Jesus.

A visiting missionary was speaking at our little church, and Elizabeth and I were sitting right down in the front row. He spoke about the need for men to carry the Word into the primitive areas of the world. At the conclusion of his presentation, he said, "I know that all the people here tonight have been saved, but have you truly made Jesus the Lord of your lives? Have you really surrendered everything to the Lord?"

It suddenly hit me that I hadn't done what he was asking. I'd done everything else. I'd invited Jesus into my heart and I'd been filled with the Spirit, but I hadn't made Him the absolute Lord of my life. Three weeks before this, Elizabeth's aunt and uncle had started leading me toward this goal, but my attitude had been, "With Jesus in my heart, what more do I need?" I was perfectly happy with the way I was. After we'd prayed, they'd tell me my growth depended on having and claiming the power of the Holy Spirit, but my head-knowledge told me that I already had everything there was to get. Man alive, was I wrong!

I knew I'd been baptized with the Holy Ghost. This aunt and uncle, together with a full-blooded Cherokee woman friend of theirs, had prayed and led me to the baptism. On the way home from a prison farm visit, they'd taken me to the church and had me kneel at the altar in my shirt sleeves, completely relaxed, to pray for the infilling of the Holy Ghost. I'd done it, and I knew the Spirit was in me.

Kneeling at that altar with my head thrown back and my arms in the air, I'd seen a ball of holy fire come to me. At first it looked like a small red marble, but as it got closer it began to take the shape of a spinning blade of fire. As I continued praising God and praying, it hung over my head but it wouldn't settle down on me.

At that point, I seemed to separate into two people. I was looking down at myself. In my heart, I'd reserved three things that I hadn't surrendered to God. As if it were a news bulletin appearing on a television screen, the first of these things passed before my eyes. I gave it up! Then the second appeared and I made another surrender. The third appeared and I turned it over to Jesus.

I heard the voice in my heart say, "Not unless you come as a little child," and I watched that figure of me at the altar shrink to child-size. The spinning wheel of flame settled down on me! I was filled with the Holy Ghost, and I knew it!

There wasn't anything left for me to give to God? I was wrong! I still hadn't made Him the total Lord of my life! I'd received the baptism of fire, but I still wasn't completely surrendered to God! I came out of that baptism speaking in tongues, but I wasn't completely His!

Now, I was hearing this missionary call me to the final surrender. Looking at Elizabeth beside me, I asked her if she'd go to the altar with me. She answered, "Yes," and with me bawling like a baby, we went forward together.

I don't remember seeing anyone else at the altar, but I'm sure that others had answered the man's call. Holding my wife's hand, I stood there and waited. The congregation started singing a hymn which contained the words, "I'll go where You want me to go, I'll do what You want me to do and I'll say what

You want me to say."

The missionary looked me right in the eyes and said, "If you don't mean that with all your heart, then don't you sing it!" He added, "It's better never to have made a vow than to make one and then break it!"

Right then, I was ready to go to Africa. I couldn't afford it, but if that's where God wanted me, then that's where I'd go. I was ready to do anything for Jesus, and I knew He'd find a way to pay for it. I sang that song, and gave myself to God in prayer, with every fiber of my being. I never dreamed just how completely God would test my conviction.

Nothing happened for six months, but one evening my little five-year-old daughter Carole came to me complaining of a pain in her stomach. When I'd made that final surrender, I'd meant it. We'd forgotten about doctors and put them aside in our total trust of the Lord. Carole had already accepted Jesus as her Savior and received the baptism of the Holy Ghost. She had her prayer language and was a believing child of God.

She was constantly having these pains in her stomach and when she'd come to me, I'd lay hands on her and ask Jesus for a healing. Her bright little smile always followed those prayers and she was healed, but this time it was different. Carole went back to bed, but she wasn't healed.

The next morning she had a temperature of 100 degrees. I prayed for her once again, and before leaving for the office, I called for the elders of the church to come and pray for her, just as the Bible instructs us to do. The preacher and one of the elders came and prayed for her. Carole's temperature was 101 when I got home that night. She looked so small and helpless in her bed when I prayed for her that evening. She awoke the next day with a temperature of 102!

Holding her in my arms, I watched her vomit blood and fear

filled my heart. Her stomach was cramping, and I could see the pain in her eyes. We hadn't given her one bit of medicine of any kind. We were trusting the Lord to answer our prayers. Once more, I prayed for her healing and called for the elders to return.

I fasted that day and when I came home, Carole's temperature was 103! Doubt began to eat at my faith. She was getting worse and I was helpless. I'd been witnessing to the man living next door and I knew if anything happened to Carole, he'd have me in court. He didn't like having me press my faith on him. He didn't believe in all this and was extremely critical of everything I did. Once more, I asked Jesus to heal her and we went to bed.

The following morning, her temperature was 104! We prayed again and I called for the elders. All day long I fasted and prayed. That evening when I returned, she was up to 105! She was so weak she couldn't even walk to the bathroom. Her little head and body were on fire!

Standing outside her bedroom door, I told Elizabeth, "Honey, I'm afraid. I've trusted God as far as I can. He hasn't healed her, and my faith is gone. With a temperature of 105, she could weaken her heart and suffer for it the rest of her life."

Nodding her head, Elizabeth agreed.

"Call Dr. McNeil," I told her, and she hurried to the phone.

The doctor agreed to meet us at his office and we bundled Carole into the car and drove over as if the Devil himself were snapping at our heels. I carried her inside and laid her on his examining table. He checked her thoroughly and turned to me in alarm.

"My God, Tommy, why haven't you brought her to me before this?"

I tried to explain about our faith and the commitment we'd

made to God, but he sadly shook his head.

"Tommy, you could lose her," he said. "She's a very sick little girl." He wrote out a prescription and handed it to me, saying, "Get this filled and follow my directions exactly. Give it to her as fast as you can. You could still lose her!"

We drove straight to the pharmacy and when I stopped the car the voice in my heart asked, "Tommy, why didn't you trust Me a little longer?"

I answered, "God, I did trust You. Why didn't You heal her? We waited five days for You to act. Why didn't you do it?"

My patience was gone. I ordered the prescription and just as I was paying for it, that voice once again spoke. "Tommy, why didn't you trust Me a little longer?"

All the way home, I continued to argue with God. Going up the front steps with Carole in my arms, I was asked again, "Tommy, why didn't you trust Me a little longer?"

I didn't even bother to answer. My daughter was sick and possibly dying. I had the prescription that could save her, and she was going to get it. Elizabeth ran to the kitchen, getting a spoon and a glass of water while I carried Carole to her room.

Pouring out a spoonful of the pink medicine, we gave it to her with a small swallow of water. It didn't stay down. It came right back up, and Elizabeth asked, "Daddy, what are we going to do?"

"Pour another spoonful," I ordered.

She did, and we tried again. It came up faster than it went down.

That voice returned. "Tommy, why didn't you trust Me a little longer?"

Everything we tried to get that medicine inside her failed. Once again God framed His question. I was sick of hearing Him ask it. My daughter was dying, and I couldn't get the medicine that would save her to stay down. In anger, I yelled, "Because You didn't heal her!"

In desperation, I carried Carole to her bed and laid her down. Elizabeth stood at the door with the medicine in her hands, weeping and pleading for the life of our daughter. Tears were streaming down my cheeks. I was full of condemnation. I'd waited too long before going to the doctor. Carole's system couldn't accept the medicine. God couldn't get through to me. I wasn't listening any longer.

As weak as she was, Carole raised up on one of her elbows and pleaded, "Daddy, if you'll pray for me one more time, Jesus will heal me."

My faith was gone, but Carole's tiny voice seemed to restore enough of it for me to pull myself together. I started praying and with every word, my voice grew stronger.

"God," I said, "I'm going to kneel here beside this bed until You heal my daughter. If I have to stay here forever, then I'll do it!"

"Please, Daddy," Carole pleaded.

Our eyes met and her faith rekindled mine. I felt the power of the Holy Spirit growing in me! "God," I prayerfully demanded, "I want you to heal Carole right now!" My hand was on her little stomach, and I hadn't finished speaking before I felt her fever begin to fall. With the complete trust and understanding of a child, Carole looked up at me and smiled. Raising herself on her elbows, she confirmed God's miracle!

"Daddy," she murmured, "Jesus has healed me. I'm hungry."

All of a sudden, I was aware of my own breathing. I began praising God and giving thanks for His miracle. Elizabeth's voice joined mine. Carole's tiny voice seemed to hang in the air with a power of its own.

"Thank You, Jesus," she said. "But, Daddy, I'm hungry."

Elizabeth questioned me with her eyes and asked, "What shall we do?"

I answered by asking Carole, "What would you like to eat?"

"Bacon and eggs, toast and milk," she happily proclaimed. Elizabeth asked, "Do you think she should have all that?"

"Go fix it," I said.

Carole got out of bed, and I held her robe. We went to the kitchen, and she ate everything we put before her. She was healed, but my understanding of it all was still to come.

# Chapter 9
# DESTINATION ATLANTA

*"For they that are after the flesh do mind the things of the flesh; but they that are after the Spirit the things of the Spirit."*
**Romans 8:5**

I know that many people will say that we were foolish in not taking Carole to the doctor immediately. Some might say that in our attempts to give her the medicine, she retained enough of it to accomplish her healing. Others might observe that our faith was weak; after asking God to heal her, we didn't believe she was healed and continued to pray. Let me put it this way: Carole knew when she was healed and she knew Who had healed her. It took me a long time to realize it, but I think God was testing me.

She was my pride and joy. In my eyes, she was an angel. Carole was my "Isaac." Just as God commanded Abraham to sacrifice his only son, I was tested. The Lord could have taken Carole, but He didn't. I don't think it was ever His intention to do so. God wanted to see how far I'd go before finally surrendering everything to Him. The moment I turned away from the answers of the flesh, He honored my prayer. I was driven away from my faith, only to learn that in the end I was helpless and had to depend on Him.

I don't want anyone to misunderstand me. Doctors are also servants of God. They are gifted with a powerful healing ministry. The advancements in the medical arts are from God. We should never judge their ministry unworthy of our use and support. Whenever I or any members of my family are ill, we always submit the illness to God for healing and then wait for His answer. Many times, we've been told to go to the doctor, and we do. The important thing is that we wait on the Lord and then obey Him. He knows what's needed better than we, and He always answers.

That first morning, when Carole wasn't healed, I should have waited for God's answer, but I didn't. My spiritual pride was in command. I'd asked for the healing in the name of Jesus and hadn't listened to see if God had something else in mind. I considered myself so spiritually wise that I knew the mind of God. I had put God in a box and figured that I knew how to use Him. The burning away of that stupid pride was part of my testing. As I said, my understanding of all this didn't come right away, and God had to continue testing me.

Months passed and the Lord continued to bless my life and family. At work, everything was running in top form. I was earning a top salary and receiving a bonus of 5 percent of all the bakery division profits. My division was the company's most profitable division. I'd refused a vice president's title because it would have meant losing my bonus. I was executing every stock option. My home was paid for, and Elizabeth had furnished it beautifully. My church work had blossomed gloriously and I was greatly respected both at home and in the secular world. I had a "bird's nest on the ground," and I knew it. Life was sweet and getting sweeter, but the voice in my heart was beginning to whisper things I didn't want to hear.

One day I was having lunch by myself in the cafeteria at the store headquarters when a total stranger tapped my shoulder. "I'm Bill Carroll from Atlanta, Georgia," he said. "I was praying yesterday, and God told me you're the man to come and work for me and run my business."

Now, God hadn't told me anything about moving to Atlanta, and if He had, I'm not sure I'd have listened. I'd offered my life to Him and I was always asking Him what He wanted me to do, but going to Atlanta wasn't one of them. I looked this guy up and down, wondering if he was some kind of nut. I'd heard stories about false prophets and such, and this man could very easily fit in that category. He didn't look like one, but then they never do. I'd heard "God said" before, but that didn't necessarily mean that it was really Him talking. Mr. Carroll had gotten my attention, but little else.

"Mr. Carroll," I said, "if you want to wait until I've finished my lunch, maybe we can discuss your proposition."

He didn't want to wait. He pulled out a chair and sat down at my table. "Mr. Ashcraft, I own the Carroll Baking Company in Atlanta. I'm a Spirit-filled Presbyterian and I want to go fulltime for the Lord. I need you to run my business!"

I nodded my understanding to this point, and he continued talking while I stared down at my chicken-fried steak. He told me how he'd asked all the bakery supply salesmen who called on him to be on the lookout for a good manager. It seems that I'd witnessed to one of these men in my office, and he'd given Carroll my name. I tried to eat, but Bill Carroll had ruined my lunch. Hoping he'd understand just how impolite I considered him to be, I pushed my half-eaten lunch away and got to my feet.

"Mr. Carroll, since you can't wait, I suggest that we discuss this in my office."

Still talking, he followed me out of the cafeteria. "My wife and I," he said, "were praying about all this yesterday morning. I put your name and three others on a sheet of paper, closed my eyes and asked God to tell me which one He wanted." Grabbing my shoulder, he stopped me on the stairs and looked me

directly in the eyes. "God guided my finger to *your* name!"
That did it. I knew this man was a nut. Turning away from
his smiling face, I charged on up the stairs. I wanted the security
of my office. I wanted him on my turf before straightening him
out. He was right behind me, talking a mile a minute when I
closed my office door. He was telling me how he and his wife
had driven straight from Atlanta to tell me the good news.
Pointing to a chair, I asked him to sit down and then went to
my desk. We stared at each other in silence for a couple of
seconds before I started talking.

"Now, let's get something straight," I said. "I have no
intention of quitting this job and moving to Atlanta. God may
have told all this to you, but He hasn't said a thing to me!"

"He will!" Bill observed.

"Look," I said, "I'm running the best bakery operation in
Texas. My bonus is growing every year. I'm a stockholder in
this company. My family's happy here in Houston." Spreading
my arms to include everything in sight, I declared, "All of this is
from God. What makes you think He wants me to walk away
from it?" I leaned forward and added, "God's given me a
ministry in my church. He's guided me to the prison farm to
help save souls. He's sent people to me for prayer." I leaned
back in my chair. "What makes you think He wants me in
Atlanta?"

Bill stood and placed both hands on my desk. Our eyes were
locked on each other. His voice started as a low rumble, but
gained volume as he spoke. "God told me He wanted you to run
my bakery. Before you say no, I suggest that you pray about
it!"

"Okay," I said, "I'll pray about it, and when God tells me to
move to Atlanta, I'll call you and let you know I'm on my
way."

"That's good enough for me," he concluded. "I'll be waiting for your call."

I had Bill's business card on my desk, but the first few days after his visit, I was kept very busy. As each day passed, the importance of praying about his request grew dimmer. Elizabeth and I talked about it, but she didn't want to leave Houston, so Atlanta faded from our thinking. I knew if God wanted me to give up everything and move, He'd tell me so in no uncertain terms. I was about to learn that God speaks to us in many ways.

Thirty days had passed when Bill Carroll called me. He wanted to know what I was doing about God's command. When I told him that I still hadn't received any word on the move, he asked me to keep praying and hung up.

Another 30 days rolled by, and he called again. This time, he was more insistent. I told him that I'd just gotten a raise, and he said he'd meet it. I told him that God hadn't said a word to me, and he asked, "Tom, are you sure you're listening?"

I was sure of one thing. I didn't need anyone to tell me how to listen to the Lord, but Bill wouldn't let it drop. Elizabeth and I were planning to visit my sister in South Carolina, and we'd be going through Atlanta. In desperation, I finally conceded, "Bill, we'll stop and visit your bakery on our way. I'll give you my answer then."

He agreed and told me he'd make reservations for us at a nearby motel. I figured I could look over his operation and tell him no, and that would be the end of it. Before breaking off his phone call, he said something that really hit me.

"Tom," he confided, "every day since our visit in Houston, I've prayed about this, and every day God has told me that you're my man."

I hadn't been praying every day about it. As far as I was

concerned, I wasn't moving to Atlanta. I couldn't conceive of God wanting me to leave the nest He'd given me. It just wasn't possible. I knew God wouldn't bless me the way He had, only to have me leave it. I'd met people who'd pulled up stakes and moved, thinking it was what God wanted, only to find out that it was all a terrible mistake. That wasn't going to happen to me! There really was no need for me to pray about it, so I hadn't. I hadn't been standing around waiting for God's command, either.

Elizabeth and I arrived in Atlanta on the Fourth of July, 1954. After getting Tommy Jr., Shirley and Carole in their swimming suits, with Elizabeth watching them from poolside, I called Bill Carroll. He sounded happy to hear my voice and invited me to visit his plant, saying, "It's closed down today, but I'll meet you there in 20 minutes." He told me how to find it, and I was on my way.

When I knew I was going to be visiting his bakery, I'd asked every salesman that called on me about it. The Carroll Baking Company was a high quality, home delivery operation. It was an old-line, family owned business. Being a graduate of the American Institute of Baking, I knew I'd be able to judge the operation once I'd seen the plant.

From the outside, the two-story building looked very impressive, but inside, it was a baker's nightmare. Every principle of baking efficiency had been violated. As Bill led me through the building, I could see where man-hours were lost by the illogical arrangement of the equipment. I knew the formulas that led to baking profits, but I couldn't see a single sign of them in the physical setup of his plant. It had grown in spite of itself and the growth had been added without any consideration of total plant efficiency.

We were sitting in his office when he said, "Tom, I need you here. When can you come to work?" He smiled and continued, "I can match the salary you're getting and I'll give you a bonus of 5 percent of the profits."

"Bill," I asked, "can I see your P. & L. Statement?" He got out the one for 1953 and handed it to me. He'd lost a lot that year. Five percent of nothing is nothing, I said to myself, and asked, "How about the first six months of this year?"

He handed it to me with a rueful smile. It was worse than the year before. He was already showing a loss of almost the same amount. He was doing a million-dollar volume each year with 65 house-to-house routes. I shook my head and said, "Even without a bonus, I don't think you can afford me."

"I can't afford to pay your moving expenses, but I'll meet your salary." A note of pleading entered his voice. "Tom, it's what God wants, and we have to obey."

"Bill, let's be practical," I said. "There's nothing about this job that makes me want to take it, but I'll tell you what I'll do. Elizabeth and I will go on up to South Carolina and I'll stop by on our way back and tell you yes or no."

He nodded his acceptance of this and invited us to dinner. I asked him to follow me back to the motel and meet my wife and family. After a short visit, we all got in his car and he drove us all over Atlanta. He showed us the fine homes that were available, the schools and the downtown district. We had dinner at a fancy steak house and then watched the holiday fireworks in the park before returning to the motel.

After he'd left, I told Elizabeth what a terrible mess his bakery was and that seemed to settle it. The next morning, Bill was at our door to guide us out of town to the right road to South Carolina. We waved goodbye and headed north.

Driving along, all I could think of was his bakery. In my mind, I rearranged all the equipment according to the formulas I knew so well. Suddenly, it dawned on me that God was using me to solve Bill's baking problems. He was showing me what must be done! The oven had to be lengthened. Bigger mixers had to be installed. The floors had to be leveled and smoothed. The flour-handling capacity had to be increased. Another bread wrapping machine was needed. All the conveyor systems had to be rearranged. God was allowing me to lay out the perfect bakery. I silently protested, "No. God, I don't want to go to Atlanta. I don't want to run that bakery. Take these thoughts out of my mind. Let me forget about Bill and his problems."

We planned to spend seven days with my sister, but the first six were among the most miserable of my life. Every time I lay down, I was putting that bakery together. Every time I was alone, the vision of the work to be done crowded in on me. I don't care what I was doing, that bakery haunted me. I couldn't even be civil to those around me. God was giving me the full treatment. I wasn't doing what He wanted, and He was letting me know about it.

On the sixth day, I went to Elizabeth and said, "Honey, get packed. We're going back to Atlanta, and I'm telling Bill that we're moving. I can't sleep, I can't eat, I can't do anything without that bakery coming to mind. God must want me to go back to the bakery!"

Bill greeted me with open arms and led the way to his office. We studied each other for several minutes before he asked, "Tom, what's it going to be?"

"It's going to cost you $200,000 to rebuild this operation, but if you'll put up the money and get out of the way while I do it, I'll come to Atlanta in 60 days, and we'll get started." I grinned at his surprise and added, "God has shown me what must be done to make this company profitable, but now you have to agree or it's no deal."

He agreed to raise the money, and we shook hands on it. I had two months to quit my job, sell our house and move to Atlanta. Knowing it wasn't going to be easy, we headed for Houston. Elizabeth tried one last time to change my mind.

"Daddy, are you sure God wants us to move?"

All three children chimed in from the back seat. They didn't want to leave their friends in Houston. In my mind, I was trying to sort out the ways I could tell my employer I was leaving, but I had to answer my wife and family.

"Yes, honey, I'm sure it's what God wants." Continuing to drive, I tried to explain. "All the time that Bill was praying and I wasn't, the Lord let me stew in my own indecision. He knew what would eventually happen and was willing to wait for me to learn the truth. Since I wasn't asking for His opinion, He wasn't giving it. That in itself should have been enough answer for me, but I had to learn the hard way, so He let me."

"That's all I wanted to know," Elizabeth conceded and started selling the kids on the idea.

The Hinke-Pillot people didn't want me to leave. They offered me a whopping big raise, which I had to refuse. We put our house on the market and waited. We had flocks of people come and look, but no buyers. We'd set the price at $31,000 and were willing to come down $2,000, but still no buyers. We didn't even receive an offer. Elizabeth had completed the packing, but three days before departure, we still owned the house.

I got on my knees and said, "Lord, do You want me to move and leave this house vacant? Am I going to have to rent it and worry about it? If You're in this move with us, then I want to sell this house."

It was listed with a real estate firm. He'd advertised and pulled out all the stops, but nothing had happened. I took it out of his hands and put up my own sign on the front lawn. On the third day, I said, "Okay, Lord, You've got one day left and right now I'm disgusted with this whole deal. I'm not even going to show the place, and I'm not going to worry about it. It's Your house, Lord; You sell it!" I even increased the price by $1,000. I left and went to the bakery to say goodbye to my friends.

About two that afternoon, Elizabeth called. "Daddy, there's a man here to see the house. It's a complete mess. Should I show it to him?"

"Yeah, go ahead," I said, " but stay firm on our new price. If he wants it, he'll have to pay $32,000 for it."

Thirty minutes later, she called back and said, "He wants it." She laughingly added, "I've accepted his $500 deposit. He's a friend of yours, and his office is right across the street from yours."

My buyer was the sales manager of a competitive bakery. We had coffee together almost every day of the week. He was buying my house for a thousand dollars more than I expected, and I didn't have to pay a real estate commission. Bill Carroll couldn't pay my moving expenses, so God had made other arrangements. We closed the deal, watched the movers load the furniture, waved goodbye to the neighbors, and drove out of Houston. God must have laughed at the antics of the Ashcrafts, but once again, the lesson was pressed home. If I would just trust Him, He'd lead me in His own way. Bill and his $200,000 were waiting for me in Atlanta and I was about to start another lesson.

# Chapter 10
# SOMETHING FOR BUSINESSMEN

*"With good will doing service, as to the Lord, and not to men:"*

**Ephesians 6:7**

Arriving in Atlanta, we quickly got settled in our new home and I turned my attention to the bakery. What had to be done was clear to me, and Bill soon saw the complete logic of what God had told me to do. Bill stepped back and gave me total authority to proceed. Together, we turned the whole enterprise over to Jesus. We made Him Chairman of the Board.

Under this new management, it was only a matter of three months until all the needed changes were completed and in operation. In November, 1954, the bakery broke even for the first time in over 30 months. The following December, it showed its first profit and our sales volume began to climb with the increased quality and freshness of our products. Bill was out working for Jesus, and I was running His bakery. We started 1955 with a song in our hearts and the certain knowledge that we were operating in the will of the Lord.

Many people consider successful Christian businessmen as hypocrites. They think a real Christian can't have an interest in making money. In their opinion, "a true Christian has to be poor like Jesus." They don't know the Lord. They've never met Him. He isn't the Lord of their lives, and they're still listening to the lies of Satan.

Jesus isn't poor! Everything on the face of the earth belongs to

Jesus. He is more than willing, when we love Him, to allow us to share His wealth. Jesus said, "The workman is worthy of his hire." Even during His earthly walk as a man, Jesus wasn't poor. A poor man doesn't need a treasurer, and Jesus had one. Even when His treasurer Judas stole from Him, He still had enough left over to meet the needs of His followers. Jesus never made a point of claiming His wealth because He knew that everything He had belonged to His Father.

We have to approach the gaining of wealth with the same understanding. If we seek it for the glory it can bring to us, then Satan can corrupt it and make both it and us become his. Jesus' wealth must be used for God's glory! We must remember that Satan knows the scriptures better than we. He can twist God's Word and, if we're weak in our faith, use it to make us his slaves. The Devil can cite the story of "The Rich Young Ruler," and, if we believe his lies, make it appear that God doesn't love a wealthy man.

When Jesus said, "And again I say unto you, it is easier for a camel to go through the eye of a needle than for a rich man to enter into the kingdom of God," He was pointing out the extreme difficulty of having wealth without worshiping it. The rich young ruler came to Jesus seeking praise for his self-righteousness, and the Lord put him to the ultimate test. If any man considers his wealth to be of greater value than the love of God, then he cannot enter the kingdom of heaven. If he's willing to forsake the commandments of God to gain wealth, and to keep it, then he is a servant of Satan. No man can love God with all his heart, soul and mind, and love his neighbors as himself, and still use whatever wealth he possesses for his own glory!

That's why the gifts of the Holy Spirit are so vital to a man of God. One of the spiritual gifts is discernment, and with this gift, man will know how and where to use his wealth for the glory of God. Jesus allowed the bakery to prosper, because Bill and I were submitted to Him. We were using the profits for His glory.

About mid-January, 1955, I received a phone call from Houston that would eventually lead to a complete change in my life. It was from A.C. "Andy" Sorelle. His voice carried over the phone line with a positive, natural assurance.

"Tom, I've found something which I think you'll really be interested in. I know what you want to do, and this will be right down your alley."

"Go on," I urged.

"I've met a man named Demos Shakarian. He's had an exciting vision from God, and when I heard it, I immediately thought of you over in Atlanta. Demos is forming an organization to bring businessmen to Jesus."

I'd been part of bringing Andy to the baptism of the Holy Spirit, and I loved him as a brother. He was a wealthy Houston oilman and a beautiful servant of the Lord. His life had been turned around, and Jesus was the Lord of his life. He owned a private airplane, and that was also available for God's work. If something excited Andy, knowing him as I did, then it excited me.

"Keep talking," I said.

"Demos is forming chapters," Andy explained, "of what he calls the Full Gospel Business Men's Fellowship International, and we want you to help us get a chapter started in Atlanta."

This was exactly what I wanted to hear. There had long been a question in my mind: Where were the businessmen of God when I needed them? Why did I have to serve Satan so long when there were surely men of God around me who could have helped? Andy's next words pointed the direction I should go to help answer these questions.

"We want you to call a group of men together over there, and then we'll fly over and help you get it organized."

That's all I needed to hear. We set a date for our first meeting, said goodbye, and I took the bit in my teeth and ran with it. Our first meeting was held later that month at Mammy's Shanty on Peachtree Street at eight o'clock in the morning. By four o'clock that same afternoon, we were off and running. They made me the temporary chairman of the new chapter and I held that office for five years. I'd gotten 67 men to attend, and every one of them signed up for a membership. They were presidents of flour mills, insurance companies, doctors, lawyers, store managers or owners and even a sprinkling of judges and politicians.

That was one of the most spiritual meetings I've ever attended. This was the start of the Atlanta Chapter, and God was involved in everything we did. It was a new and exciting experience for all of us. We felt the love of God and openly demonstrated that same love for each other. We learned the joy of being free to proclaim our faith openly in the business community. Every one of us knew other men who needed this same freedom. Each of us knew someone who needed Christian fellowship to strengthen their faith in their daily lives.

Too many businessmen leave God in their churches on Sunday, because they're afraid people won't understand Him in their businesses. They've listened to Satan's lies too long and some of them even consider themselves as being like the "money-changers" in the Temple! The Full Gospel Business Men's Fellowship International strikes right at the heart of this falsehood! It disproves the Devil's lies and throws them back in his foul face! Satan hates us because we no longer believe him! Jesus is alive and well in our lives and our businesses!

Before someone says, "That's all well and good for you,

Tommy Ashcraft, but it won't work in my business," let me set them straight. If any man truly gives his business to God, He'll honor that gift, and it's impossible to outgive God! If you merely give lip-service to this principle, God will not honor it, and the Devil will take over! The surrender has to be complete, and the Lord has to be first in all things, or failure will be the eventual reward. If whatever is done is for the glory of God, it cannot fail! But beware of worshiping success to the exclusion of the Lord!

The sole purpose of the Full Gospel Business Men's Fellowship International is to provide a forum for Christian witness. The organization is not a church. Theology isn't taught at the meetings. The chapters have no liturgy and offer no sacraments. Ministers, preachers, pastors and priests can belong to the organization, but they can't hold office. They can give witness of what God has done in their lives. The FGBMFI is a layman's organization. It's nondenominational. It's a nonprofit organization that meets once a month to hear businessmen tell how the Lord has changed their lives. Wives and sweethearts are welcomed and encouraged to attend the meetings, and many have given their witness, but they're not allowed to become members. We feel the men need the help.

Membership carries no honors or privileges. It merely implies a commitment to God and nothing more. There are no second-class Christians in the hearts and minds of Full Gospel Business Men. Being a member doesn't make anyone a better Christian, but it does provide a common fellowship for those who choose to follow Jesus. We support each other in our faith and proudly admit Jesus is the Lord of our lives. Many men have found this basic truth in the Fellowship, and they experience joy in helping others come to this understanding.

This was true in Atlanta. The attendance at each successive

meeting grew. The Atlanta Chapter was the eleventh chapter
formed in the whole world. There are now more than 2,450
chapters. The members of our chapter considered it part of their
personal ministry to bring new people to every meeting. It was
glorious to see the love of the Lord blossom in the lives of the
men around me. I'm now convinced that part of the reason God
wanted me in Atlanta was to become involved in this powerful
ministry.

Today, Atlanta is the largest chapter in the world. It's not
unusual for 1,600 men to attend one of their breakfast meetings.
It still is their practice that every member should bring a guest. I
always had a guest with me, but one Saturday morning the
friend I planned on bringing couldn't attend. He had to make an
emergency trip on business and promised to come the following
month.

Sitting at the head table with a vacant chair beside me just
wasn't my cup of tea. It bothered me, and the voice in my heart
told me to get up and find someone to take my guest's place. We
were meeting at the Atlanta Biltmore Hotel at the time, so I
walked into the lobby to find someone. The lobby was empty,
and it was raining outside. After I stood there for several
minutes, the voice told me to go out on the sidewalk. I didn't
want to go out in the rain, but I obeyed.

The only person in sight was a man sitting with his back
against the building. The voice said, "There's your guest."

His head was hanging down with his long, uncut, brown hair
hanging over his face. The old brown shirt he was wearing
didn't look clean, and his ragged brown pants were water-
soaked up to his knees. There was an empty wine bottle in a
paper bag lying beside him. "Oh, Lord," I said, "not him."

"Yes, Tommy," the voice answered, "he's your guest."

I walked over and gently touched him. He looked up with

bleary eyes and little understanding of what was happening. His
beard was at least three days old, and he could hardly speak.

"What?" he stammered.

"Would you be my guest for breakfast here at the Biltmore
this morning?"

The surprise showed in his face as he looked me up and
down. "I guess so," he agreed.

I helped him to his feet and steadied him as he tried to walk. It
was a real project getting him through the revolving door, but
we finally made it. Somehow, the two of us managed to stagger
through the lobby and into the dining room. More pushing than
leading, I got him up to the head table and into the chair beside
me. The eyes of everyone in the room had followed our
wobbling progress with ill-concealed amusement. I know that
many of them thought, "What's old Tommy up to now?"

As the master of ceremonies, I didn't have a chance to learn
the man's name or give him mine. The meeting was late getting
started, and I had to get it underway. In the back of my mind
while I was speaking, the words of Jesus began to stir. "Verily I
say unto you, inasmuch as ye have done it unto one of the least
of these my brethren, you have done it unto me."

This grew stronger in my mind as we ate our breakfast. My
guest could hardly eat his bacon and eggs. He fed his chin and
nose more than his mouth, but, wobbly neck and all, he finally
got it down.

When our speaker was finished, I got to my feet and issued
the usual invitation. "Is there anyone here this morning who
would like to meet our Lord Jesus? If you're having trouble in
your business or home, mind or body, now's the time to come
forward."

My guest was the first to raise his hand. He actually shook it
right in my face. He was sitting right beside me, and I couldn't

overlook him. Lee Watson, one of my best friends, was sitting on the other side, and I turned to him. "Lee, get over there and pray with this man."

Grinning with absolute delight, Lee went to work. He knelt beside my guest's chair and prayed him through to Jesus. We all watched a miracle take place. When my guest claimed his salvation, he stood on his feet completely sober. He didn't look the same. He was a new man. There was victory in his eyes.

The meeting was over when I finally got to meet my guest. He told me an amazing tale. Two years before, he'd been a respected Atlanta businessman. He'd started drinking, and his wife had left him. She got half his business in the divorce settlement, and in remorse he'd drunk the other half. He couldn't hold a job, and skid row became his home. Looking at him as he sobbed out his story, I could almost see myself and what I might have become if I hadn't received God's grace. His eyes were filled with glorious light when he finally said, "But, Mr. Ashcraft, I have received a new heart this morning and all that's behind me!" He was smiling with confidence when he added, "I'm going to get my wife and children back!"

Before I left Atlanta, I watched this man regain everything he'd lost. His wife and family returned. He got his business back, and he's now taking guests of his own to the chapter meetings. That man also had a great effect on my life. In the miracle of his salvation, I saw the complete truth and beauty of Demos Shakarian's vision. Jesus used it to confirm to me the direction He wanted me to take.

With the approval, support and help of Bill Carroll, I began turning the baking company into a ministry. Bill opened his big office for Friday night prayer meetings, and people from all over Atlanta soon began coming. Ministers and pastors even brought their problems to the Lord in the quiet, secure confines of these meetings. Jesus was there, and nothing was beyond solution.

All the time this was taking place, the profits of the bakery continued to grow. The first year showed a net profit of $152,000. It increased every year, and after just five years we were clearing over $450,000. We were going for the Lord, and He was blessing us with a glorious victory. Where we once served just the city of Atlanta, the Carroll Baking Company was now serving half the state. Two hundred trucks rolled daily with our products, and God enabled us to provide jobs and incomes for almost five times the company's previous peak employment.

Everyone knew Jesus was the Chairman of the Board. We sponsored ministers on the radio and made no bones about our love for God. We glorified Him, and He blessed us!

The nest God had given me in Houston was completely forgotten. If Houston was a comfortable nest, Atlanta was becoming a palace. I was being fulfilled, and a great sense of ministry was settling over me. My 5 percent of the profits was making it possible for me to devote more time to God, and my family was enjoying the same degree of success and comfort. The Full Gospel Business Men's chapter was growing, and we were seeing great miracles of salvation and healing. It never occurred to any of us that all this might not be in the complete will of God. Sometimes it's necessary for the Lord to teach us the same lesson twice. At least, it was necessary with me, because I'd gone to nest again.

Elizabeth, the children and I had taken to Atlanta like ducks take to water. We'd pulled the security of success up around our necks and snuggled into the creature comforts of life. In doing this, we hadn't realized how great the limitations were that we'd placed on ourselves and the way God could use us. We were still asking God to let us serve Him, but now we expected that service to be at our convenience. He was of an entirely different frame of mind!

One morning, about midyear, 1962, Mr. Carroll came into my office and sat down. I was on the phone with one of our suppliers, and he waited for me to complete the call before speaking.

"Tom," he said, "I'm 73 years old. I have no children, and this business is getting too big for me. I'm going to sell out." Smiling at the surprise he must have seen in my face, he added, "I wanted you to be the first to know."

I started to protest, but another thought entered my mind. "Mr. Carroll," I said, "if you've really decided to sell, I'd like to buy. How much are you asking?"

"One million dollars," he softly replied.

I didn't have that kind of money, but figured I could raise it and asked him to give me a couple of days' time. He agreed and left my office. I scraped the bottom of every available barrel for the next two days. When everything possible had been considered, my banker and I could only come up with $750,000. I was still a quarter of a million short. I laid it out for Bill Carroll and asked, "Perhaps you can carry the balance?" Bill's wisdom and experience were evident in his answer.

"No, Tom, buying the bakery that way, you'd work yourself to death and all the joy we've achieved would be lost. I'd be letting you hang a millstone around your neck."

"We could give it a try," I suggested.

He shook his head and said, "I've got buyers with the cash, and that's the way I'm going."

"Who?" I asked.

"The Clark brothers," he answered. "Their daddy was an old friend of mine, and they're my lawyers. Their wives came to see me yesterday, and I told them about you being first in line. We agreed that if you couldn't come up with the cash, I'd sell to them. It's done, Tommy, and I pray there's no hard feeling."

I wanted the bakery in the worst way, but God had made it impossible for me to buy. My employment contract still had two years to run, and I figured I could be a lot worse off, but that wasn't in the Lord's plans. My first meeting with the new owners was a revelation.

The youngest of the Clarks was a feisty little guy, and he'd never really taken to me. The oldest brother was a diabetic, and I'd prayed for his healing, but on this occasion they were of the same mind. Calling me into Mr. Carroll's office, they made it very clear they didn't want me around.

As soon as I got settled in a chair, young Walter rose to his feet and declared, "Mr. Ashcraft, we're not going to be needing you around here any longer. This bakery is so well organized that we can save your salary."

I looked him and his brother in the eyes before replying, "What about my contract? Are you going to buy it off?"

"No, sir," the older brother answered. "That contract is with Mr. Carroll, and we don't know what he intends doing about it."

"I'm sorry, gentlemen," I pressed, "but my contract is with the Carroll Baking Company, and you're going to honor it."

"No way!" Walter shouted. "But there is one thing you can do for us while you're clearing out."

"What's that?" I asked.

"When you come to work in the morning," he grimly said, "we want you to leave your Jesus in the parking lot! When you go home at night, pick Him up and take Him with you! This is a business, and there'll be no more Jesus or prayer meetings around here!"

Both of these men were church-goers. They knew who Jesus

is, and having handled Bill's legal affairs for so long, they knew how he felt about the Lord. Looking at the greed in their faces, I silently cried for their souls. It was almost as if I were seeing myself, and the kind of man I'd been just a few years before. God nudged me to my feet with a word of prophecy.

Pointing at them, I said, "If you take Jesus out of this business, you'll lose everything within a year!" Their cocky, self-confident smiles were the only reactions I received. (A little over a year later, the bakery went broke). I gave them something else to think about. "And as for my contract, I'm not leaving the company until it's settled in full!" It never occurred to me that perhaps God wanted me out of there.

As soon as I left their meeting, I called and made an appointment to see my attorneys, Lynwood Maddox and Kermit Bradford. They were active in the Full Gospel Business Men's chapter, and we'd been close friends from the start. After explaining the situation to them, I waited for their advice. It, too, was a revelation.

"I think you've got them where the hair is short," Lynwood said, "but we'd rather not get involved. Bill Carroll's a dear friend, and this could get very dirty."

"What should I do?" I asked.

"We know just the man for you," Kermit answered. "Mr. Jebb Robert Black, the meanest man in Atlanta, is the man you'll need."

They took me down and introduced me to Jebb. On the way, they explained how Black never gave up on a case. He was a tiger in every legal sense, and his reputation meant trouble for anyone opposing him in a court of law. Jebb was a tobacco-chewing hard case, and after hearing the details of my problem, he could hardly wait to handle it.

"Mr. Ashcraft," he joyfully announced, "I've wanted to get

the Clark brothers for a long time." Smiling with total pleasure, he rubbed his hands together and said, "I'll get you a million dollar settlement!"

"No," I protested. "All I want is what I have coming."

"And you'll get it," he soothingly assured, "plus a lot extra to compensate for the trouble they've caused."

Saying, "I'll have to think about it," I led Kermit and Lynwood out of Jebb's office.

As I rode the elevator down to the street, my mind was in turmoil. I didn't want to cause a lot of trouble. I wasn't rich, but I wasn't hurting for money. My reputation in the baking industry was good, and I knew I'd have no trouble getting a new job. Bill Carroll would give me an excellent recommendation, and besides, I really wanted to go into business for myself. Once we were out on the sidewalk, I expressed all this to my friends, and they came up with a suggestion.

"Let's go have a meeting with the Clarks," Lynwood said. "I think I know how to get them into a different frame of mind." Kermit nodded as if he understood what Lynwood meant and added, "I have a hunch they'll make you an offer when we're through with them."

We made the appointment for the following day, and I went home to tell Elizabeth the news. I've never spent a more restless night. We prayed about it and discussed it, but regardless of what happened, we knew we were faced with a change in the life we were living. Our nest was being destroyed, and we seemed helpless to do anything about it. Placing the problem in the hands of the Lord, we agreed to accept whatever He sent us. The following morning, with Lynwood beside me, I faced the Clarks.

"Gentlemen," I said, "I'm ready to leave any time you're ready to settle my contract."

They gave us a friendly smile and Walter Clark spoke for them. "Tom, we don't think you have a thing coming from us, but we're willing to pay $3,000 just to keep things peaceful."

"No, I think you're going to pay in full," I replied.

Clarence, the older brother, then spoke up. "Three thousand is all you're going to get. Take it or leave it."

Lynwood then dropped his bomb. "Clarence, I try to stay out of cases like this, but Tom came to me for help, and I took him over to see Jebb Black. Black's agreed to take the case, and he's going to handle it."

"How can you do such a thing?" Walter yelled. "He's the most hated lawyer in the state of Georgia. This thing will go on forever with him involved."

Clarence was of the same opinion. "Lynwood, you know the kind of man Black is. Do you really think it's Christian to bring him into this?"

The only answer they got was the famous Maddox smile, because Lynwood and I were on our way out of the office. Outside in the company parking lot, Maddox gave me one final piece of advice.

"Tom, whatever you do, don't quit. Make them fire you. That way, they'll be breaking the contract."

I figured I was already fired, but they hadn't demanded my keys, and I still had my office. Lynwood straightened me out on that and then left. The Clarks made the rest of that day pure hell for me. They kept reminding me of their "generous" $3,000 offer, and I kept turning it down. That night, during the men's prayer meeting at our church, God took a hand in the action.

In my mind I'd decided to accept a $22,000 settlement. I had a great deal more than that coming, but that amount seemed fair. I wasn't completely happy about it, and during the prayer meeting, I submitted the amount of the settlement to God. For the second time in my life, I heard the voice that had spoken to me on the church steps in Houston.

"Tom, I want you to accept $8,889!"

"Lord," I asked, "where'd You get a figure like that?" I got no explanation, so I said, "If that's what You want me to take, that's what I'll tell them."

In my mind I knew I'd settle for the figure God had set, but in my heart there was still a great deal of pain. When I'd go to the office in the morning, all my things would be stacked out in the hallway. If I spoke to one of my superintendents, and either of the Clarks was nearby, the man wouldn't speak to me. If I tried to shake hands, my hand would always remain empty. Time after time, I'd start to quit, and Lynwood's warning would come back to me. It was really the first time in my professional life that I'd felt unwanted. I was ready to leave the company on the morning after the Lord had set the amount of the settlement.

When I entered the building, I waved one of the supervisors over and gave him the message. "Tell the Clarks that I'll settle for $8,889." He nodded his understanding, and I went up to my office. The door was locked and the notice telling me that I was fired was taped to the door. I was out. They had fired me. I saw the same supervisor on my way out and repeated my message, adding, "Tell them I won't take a penny less, and if they don't agree, we're going to court."

The man delivered my message. That same day I got a phone call from an attorney for the Clarks telling me that they'd accepted my offer. He had a certified check in the amount of $8,889 waiting for me and asked if I'd pick it up before six o'clock that afternoon.

When I picked up the check, there was a glowing letter of recommendation with it. It's hard to describe the relief I felt when it was all over. I didn't know what I was going to do, but at least I knew what I wasn't going to do. I knew I wouldn't be going to court and, in all probability, I wouldn't be living in Atlanta much longer. My brother Frank had asked me to join him in starting a bakery of our own in Houston, and I decided to give the idea a lot of serious thought.

I expected Elizabeth and the children to object when I suggested moving back to Texas, but they surprised me by being all for it. After selling our house, saying goodbye to all our friends, and packing, we headed west. There was only one thing that really bothered me about leaving, and that was the fact that I'd be walking away from the Atlanta Chapter of the Full Gospel Business Men's Fellowship International. It had been my baby. I'd been its only president, and I didn't want to see it die. Without my being aware of it, Satan began speaking to my heart.

"Tom, you can't leave those guys. They won't know how to get along without you. They need you here in Atlanta. If you walk away now, it'll prove to them that you never really cared about their happiness or their lives."

That voice sounded like the Lord, but it was only the beginning of what was to come.

# Chapter 11

# MY HEAD IS A BATTLEGROUND

*"I am forgotten as a dead man out of mind: I am like a broken vessel."*

**Psalm 31:12**

The conviction that I was deserting my friends grew stronger with every mile we traveled toward Houston. Satan had found a point of vulnerability in me and was opening a wider wound. He was setting me up and pulling my eyes away from God. By the time we entered Texas, I was convinced that I'd allowed the Devil to drive me out of Atlanta. I knew I should have stayed and fought the Clarks. I knew the men I'd led to Jesus would fall away without me there to steady them. The happy laughter of my wife and children did nothing to lighten my growing burden.

It took us a few days to get settled, and then Frank and I turned our attention to forming a new bakery. My brother was already operating a small bakery of his own, and we planned to enlarge it by adding more production capacity. We offered our proposed plans up to God for His blessings and forged ahead.

Many of my old friends had welcomed me back to Houston, and through them I discovered the Rice Baking Company was for sale. By my standards, it was a small outfit but it had one advantage. As the new owner, I'd be the bakery supplier for the Rice Stores. We finalized the deal, and we were in business. Frank and I joined forces, and the Ashcraft Bakery was born. God blessed it, and it grew.

In a short time, we were running 16 trucks and building a new 10,000-square-foot plant. I was attending church every Sunday and making every Full Gospel Business Men's meeting. Elizabeth and the children took an active interest in my witnessing ministry and Carole, my youngest daughter, was adding her lovely singing voice to my presentations. From the outside, we appeared totally happy, but my heart was breaking into a thousand pieces over my desertion of Atlanta. I was convinced that I had stepped out of the will of God and was being damned for it.

For two years, my conviction grew with each passing day. I'd phone the men I knew in Atlanta and ask how things were going. They'd assure me that everything was fine, but I was certain they were lying. After each call, I'd sit at my desk and weep. Every waking hour was filled with this terrible obsession. Whenever I was alone, I'd start to cry. Trying to hide my grief from those around me, I'd stand between the trucks in our parking lot and bawl like a baby. Satan was having a field day with me, and I seemed helpless against him. I was sure God had forsaken me, because I had disappointed Him.

Elizabeth could see the hurt that was in me and when I'd ask, "Honey, do you think I'm out of God's will?", her reaction was always the same.

"No, Daddy, you're not out of God's will. God is blessing our family. He's blessing our business. He's given us a beautiful home. You're doing as much for the Lord as you ever did, and I'm sure you're not out of God's will."

Even with her reassurance, I couldn't see it. The pressure of conviction continued to build within me. I knew Satan could reward his servants and when we added the second 10,000 square feet to the bakery, I actually thought it was from the dark master of hell. My soul was in torment, and the Devil's scales encased my heart. To me, every victory I achieved became a reward from hell.

One evening, after about 18 months of this, I was sitting at the kitchen table while Elizabeth was clearing away the supper dishes. We were discussing how the children had grown; how happy Tommy Jr. was in his marriage; what a glorious lady Shirley had become; and how Carole's petite beauty was blossoming with every passing day. We were marveling over how each of them had come to love the Lord and how He was loving them. It should have been a happy time, but the pressure inside me was about to explode!

Suddenly, my legs started to steam and burn. Pain filled my chest with tendrils of agony extending down my arms. My neck felt like it was twice the size of my head. My eyeballs felt as if they were about to pop out and explode. I tried to get on my feet and failed.

Elizabeth was just closing the refrigerator door when she saw me and screamed, "Daddy, what's the matter?"

I knew I was having a heart attack, but I couldn't speak. She was standing there in terrible confusion when I finally gasped, "It's my heart!"

In that instant, God gave her supernatural strength. She got her arms under mine and half-carried me into the den. I couldn't lie down and couldn't stand. The only way I could breathe, and then with just shallow, sharp breaths, was to sit doubled over.

Seeing me in such pain, Elizabeth had the presence of mind to turn to God. She took my Bible and placed it on my back. I heard her brave voice say, "God, heal my husband! He's too young to die!"

The words were no sooner out of her mouth than I got my first deep breath. She kept the Bible on my back and continued to pray and praise God for my healing. My breathing began to normalize, and I was able to lean back on the couch. Tears of relief were streaming down her cheeks when she asked, "Daddy, what should we do?"

I knew that one heart attack could be followed by another, and I asked her to call Dr. McNeil. After making certain that I was strong enough to travel, he asked us to meet him at his office. We called Frank and his wife to meet us there and left the house with Elizabeth practically dragging me to the car. I felt weak and my heartbeat was an irregular flutter.

I know if we'd have listened, we would have heard Satan's insane laughter as we drove across town. He was giving me my reward for having listened to him, but now God was taking a powerful hand in my affairs, and the Devil would have to wait. In my mind I tried to think of anything I could have done that still remain unconfessed to God. It didn't occur to me that my doubt could be a sin, and I passed over it.

After taking my blood pressure and giving me a general examination, Dr. McNeil questioned me in detail about what had happened. In the end he concluded, "Tom, you've had an attack, there's no doubt about that, but you appear to be okay now. Your blood pressure is normal and you're weak, but I think the primary danger has passed. I want you back here in the morning for a complete physical and electrocardiogram." He prepared a hypodermic syringe while he was talking and then offered, "I'll give you a relaxing shot now, and I want you to go home to bed."

The next morning, Elizabeth got me up and dressed for my 10 o'clock appointment. I felt a little stronger and all vestiges of my pain were gone. When my examination was completed, I was once again sent home to bed. The doctor would call me when the results where in, but he was encouraged by my healthy color and my physical strengthening.

He called the next day with a note of amazement in his voice. "Tommy, I can't believe the results of your tests. The electrocardiogram came out perfect. We can't find a single scar on your heart. If you actually hadn't experienced this attack, I'd say it was all just a bad dream."

"What should I do?" I asked.

"Take it easy for a day or two, and when you feel strong enough, go back to work." He chuckled and added, "Now I don't mean for you to go back in your usual style. I want you to ease up and go back in stages. Physically, you're okay, but the attack did happen, so don't overdo it!"

Elizabeth's reaction to the good news was typically female. She was all smiles, and after seeing to my comfort, she announced, "I'm going shopping!" We were back to normal and I had the house all to myself. I now had the time to examine myself fully and where I was with the Lord.

Getting my Bible, I settled down for some time with God. "Lord," I said, "I want to know what's wrong with me. I want to know why I had this heart attack. I want to know why I've been so depressed. I want to know why I can't be alone without crying. Tell me, Lord, so that I'll understand."

I've heard of people playing "Bible roulette," where they blindly open a Bible and place their finger on a verse for guidance. I don't recommend this practice, but that's what I did. Fortunately, my finger didn't land on the verse that commands that "ye pluck out thy eye if it offends thee." My finger landed on the first verse of the 37th Psalm. The first three words I read nearly blew my mind: "Fret not thyself."

I read on and became more excited with every word. Wanting to be certain I understood the meaning of "fret," I looked it up in the dictionary: "To be irritated, annoyed or querulous; to worry." Man, that's the very thing I'd been doing, and now God was telling me to stop! Verse 3 told me what I should have been doing: "Trust in the Lord, and do good; so shalt thou dwell in the land, and verily thou shalt be fed."

The words were jumping right off the page for me! God was feeding me with His Word! He was giving me the medicine I really needed! I could hardly contain my excitement. My fretting had kept me from that which I desperately needed. I hadn't been able to see God in my life because I'd been listening to Satan's lies. The fourth verse literally boiled in front of me: "Delight thyself also in the Lord; and he shall give thee the desires of thine heart."

I hadn't been able to delight myself in the Lord for two or three years. I'd been worried because all that time I thought I was out of God's will. I thought I'd moved out of Atlanta and left all those men over there unprotected. The Devil had really jabbed me with an unholy pride. The fifth verse really stopped me. "Commit thy way unto the Lord; trust also in him, and he shall bring it to pass."

"Lord," I said, "I'm committed to You. I've given You my life. I know I'm committed to You."

The voice in my heart said, "Commit thy way!"

"You know I have, Lord," I replied, "but what does all this mean?"

"Tom," the voice asked, "did you save those men in Atlanta?"

"No, Lord, You did. I just led them to You."

"That's right," the voice said. "Those men do not belong to you! They belong to Me! I saved them, and I'll keep them." For a few moments, the silence was almost ominous in my heart and then the voice spoke again. "Commit thy way!" it commanded. "Your job is to bring men to Me! I'll do the rest!"

I can't express the joy that filled me with this renewed

understanding. I hadn't been out of the will of God; I had simply been led away from my commitment. I now knew who had been talking to me. Buckling on the armor of God, I prepared to do battle, but Satan had fled from me. My healing was complete. My strength returned, and I ceased worrying about the people I'd led to Jesus. He would take care of them better than I could ever hope to do. God had defined my job, and I had accepted it, but my testing still wasn't completed.

The next six months blossomed like a new flower. The business was booming and growing. I was traveling far and wide giving witness to the glory of God. Carole and Elizabeth were with me, and my daughter's singing was gaining power. She was becoming a beautiful asset to my ministry. Every Full Gospel chapter took her to their hearts. After hearing her sweet voice, people were flocking to the Lord. When she was introduced, more times than not, she was called an angel from heaven. She wore her petite beauty and charm like a cloak of gentle, humble grace. Her modesty was endearing, and the physical perfection of her appearance was a delicate tribute to the supreme power and glory of God.

Carole had always been the apple of her daddy's eye. I loved her to the same degree that our heavenly Father must love His Son. She was precious to me in so many ways. If she'd asked for the world, I'd have broken my back trying to get it for her, but her demands on my love were always small. I loved her more than she ever asked.

Carole was 18, just out of school, when she came to me with a special request. "Daddy," she murmured, "I want to get married. I don't want to marry one of the boys from the church. I want a man that stands six feet tall. I want him to be an officer in the Air Force and a college graduate. He must be handsome and gentle. He must also love the Lord as much as we do."

"That's a pretty tall order, darling," I answered. "But I'm sure that God can find just what you want if we ask Him."

She agreed, and we got on our knees and prayed. She laid out all her requirements and with my complete agreement, we claimed such a man for her in the name of Jesus. Both of us praised the Lord for His lovingkindness and went on about our separate ways.

The following Sunday, Carole wasn't feeling well, and we allowed her to remain home from church. I was just beginning to teach my teenage Sunday school class when in walked a six-foot second lieutenant in the United States Air Force. I could see a heavy, masculine school ring on his hand, and that spelled college. He was handsome, and in my mind's eye he was exactly what Carole and I had prayed for.

I didn't know his name, but after Sunday school was over and the worship service began, I kept my eyes on him. Following the service, he went up to the rail for prayers with me right behind him. I knelt down and prayed with him and afterwards, I introduced myself. He smiled and gave me his name.

"I'm David Franklin."

I liked the deep tone of his voice and the confidence he exuded. He was all man, and I knew he loved the Lord. Up close, I could read "Texas A. & M." embossed on his ring. "David," I said, "are you going to be here next Sunday?"

"Yes, sir," he replied, "I'll be here for the next two weeks."

"Good man," I almost roared, "I'll see you in Sunday school."

He promised to be there, and I could hardly wait to get home. Carole was still in bed when we got there, and I sat down beside her. Taking her hand in mine, I happily reported, "Honey, I met your husband this morning."

"Oh, Daddy," she exclaimed, "why wasn't I there?"

"He's exactly what we prayed for."

"Will he be there next Sunday?"

"Yep!"

Her smile was absolutely brilliant when she announced, "Then I'll be there, too, Daddy."

I'm a firm believer in fathers and daughters praying together for husbands, because God surely answered our prayer. I think it's a father's duty to lead his daughter to such prayers. It worked for us.

The following Sunday, when Carole got ready for church, she dressed with special care. She was a vision in black silk lace. Her sweet face was almost hidden under the wide brim of her black silk hat. She wore black patent leather pumps and sheer black stockings. When she emerged from her bedroom that morning, my little girl had become a beautiful lady.

When Sunday school was over the church was packed, but Carole had saved a seat beside her. David's long legs simply guided him to that seat. I introduced them, and peering under the brim of her hat, he said, "Hi, I'm David Franklin." From that point on, the end result was never in doubt.

The day after they were married, David and Carole left for the Philippines. They made David's first tour of overseas duty their honeymoon. While he was on active duty, Carole volunteered for hospital work as a nurse. It was a military hospital, and suddenly she was thrown into the harsh reality of war. It was more than her gentle, sensitive nature could stand. Having to read "Dear John" letters to men no longer able to see was too much for her. Having to comfort men with no legs and arms added a heavy burden to her soul. The continuing pressure of it broke her, and she became ill. This was compounded by the depression she felt all around her. At the end of David's tour, they came home.

Carole wasn't well, and we helped them get settled into civilian life. After a brief vacation, David came to work at the bakery as our assistant sales manager. Carole got a job as a dental nurse, and a sense of stability seemed to enter their lives. She was 23 years old, but that time in the Philippines had aged her emotionally and physically. She couldn't seem to pull away from depression.

Everything seemed to roll along smoothly for about six months, but one morning David was late getting to work, and he called me. His workday started at four o'clock in the morning, but I was still home.

"Dad, Carole is really sick, and I've got to get to work. Can you and Mother come over and get her to the hospital? The doctor will meet you there, but someone should stay with her."

Elizabeth and I really weren't aware how ill she was until that morning. Arriving at the house, we found Carole cuddled into a tight ball in her bed. It appeared as if she were seeking warmth and strength from within herself. All her glorious color was gone, and she was spitting a white froth from her mouth. I experienced the same stinging in my eyes and heart that I'd felt when I saw my mother alive for the last time.

As gently as possible, I asked, "Honey, what's wrong?"

Her voice was just a whisper. "Daddy, I'm so tired and I'm very sick."

In a matter of minutes, we were on our way to St. Luke's Hospital. After receiving her in Emergency, they immediately rushed her upstairs for X-rays. We followed along and after a short wait the doctor came out and asked if there had ever been a history of tuberculosis in the family. We assured him there hadn't, and he returned for more X-rays. In a few minutes he returned and told us they were going to hold her for observation and further tests. He suggested that we go home and return at nine o'clock in the morning. He seemed so very calm as he said, "We'll know more then and perhaps we can give you a more definite prognosis."

Elizabeth, David and I were back at the appointed time. Carole was in a private room, and the doctor was waiting for our arrival. We were shown the results. One X-ray showed her left side. The doctor's finger slowly traced the shape of the tumor growing from the top of her heart. It was egg-shaped and about the size of a grapefruit.

"We really don't know what this is," the doctor explained, "but we're going to start a series of tests to determine if it's malignant or benign."

This was the start of almost endless testing. She remained in that room for 31 days. The testing would have to stop from time to time so they could rebuild her strength. During all this time, Elizabeth and I never ceased asking God to heal her. We knew He could do anything, and we weren't afraid to ask. Elizabeth did nothing but weep and pray. She stayed at the hospital day and night. In that 31 days, my wife prayed and wept herself into a nervous breakdown.

We obtained Carole's release long enough for a fast flight to Washington, D. C., for a Kathryn Kuhlman healing service, but the Lord didn't seem to respond. Back at St. Luke's, they decided to do an exploratory operation. Every symptom pointed to cancer, but only an operation would tell us for sure. When Carole was told the news, she turned to me and asked, "Daddy, what should I do?"

"Darling," I answered, "you're of legal age, and you know the Lord. This has to be your decision. It's your body and your life."

Her faint smile told me her answer before she spoke. "God hasn't answered our prayers so far, so I'm going to let them go ahead and operate." David agreed with her decision, and it was settled.

The operation was performed that same day. They went in and lifted one of her ribs for an unblocked examination of her beating heart. After one look, they went no further. Sewing her back up, they had her transferred to Intensive Care, and the Chief Surgeon came looking for us.

"I'm sorry, folks, but there's nothing we can do. We went in and took a look. It's inoperable cancer, and it's terminal. We really don't expect her to come out of Intensive Care alive."

I couldn't accept this. God had healed her when she was just a child. He'd healed us all at one time or another, and I knew He wouldn't fail us this time. One look at my wife told me she was taking it much harder. She'd lost a lot of weight, and I was afraid she might be next. Elizabeth was desperately pressing the doctor for more information and he finally conceded, "Your daughter may live for another two weeks, but I can't truthfully say anything beyond that."

The thought that Carole's beautiful voice would no longer be heard, or that her gracious smile would no longer warm the hearts of those around her, was hard for me to take. After all, she was my Isaac, and I'd given her to God for His glory, but her death would glorify nothing. Looking down at her pale form in that terrible bed filled me with pain. My heart wanted to hear the soft echo of her songs, and my arms wanted to feel the joy of her warmth. The rise and fall of the sheet over her body was matched by the rise and fall of my spirit. Knowing that sheet could suddenly lie perfectly still sent a surge of anguish to the very core of my soul.

After the doctor left, we tried to decide who should stay with Carole. One look at Elizabeth told me she shouldn't be the one, and David was going to stay in any case, so I took my wife's hand and led her toward the exit and the car.

We drove out to Shirley's for dinner. Carole's sister was torn between grief and anxiety when she saw her mother. The news was grim and so was our mood, but Shirley fixed us a nourishing meal, and we sat down to eat. During the eating, Elizabeth left us and entered a world of grief all her own. A nervous breakdown hits suddenly, but it can linger for months. That afternoon, my wife started a 22-month walk in her own private hell.

The memory of all this had pulled tears from my eyes, and the steady drone of our aircraft's engines seemed to be singing the tender strains of "Amazing Grace." Raising my seat to its upright position, I tried to change my mood by staring out into the darkness of the night sky. A movement at the forward end of the cabin caught the corner of my eyes. Captain Porter was standing there with a tea cup in his hand, talking to someone inside the pantry. He kept looking back into the gloom of the cabin. I sensed he was looking for some sign that I was awake. Reaching up, I snapped on my reading light and waited.

It was only seconds until he flashed a smile and half salute in my direction. Reaching into the pantry, he withdrew his arms bearing a tray of sandwiches and coffee. With the sure-footed stride of an airman, he headed my way. Once again I dropped the service tray from the back of the seat in front of me. The captain was full of British good cheer as he handed me the tray and settled down beside me.

"I hope you don't mind my ordering a little snack for us." With a nod of his head, he indicated the loaded tray. "I had the girls fix us some smashing scrambled egg and sausage sandwiches." He grinned like a delighted little boy and added, "They had to strip two breakfast trays to do it, but we had a few extra so it won't matter."

I hadn't realized how hungry I was until I started eating. The sandwiches were delicious and, speaking around a mouthful of eggs and sausage, I told him so. "I was famished and these sure hit the spot."

"We're about three hours out of Houston," he said, "and I wanted to have a little chat before getting there."

Still chewing, I nodded my understanding.

"Mr. Ashcraft, I've been sitting up on the flight deck thinking about what you said earlier tonight. My wife and I both feel that going to church is a waste of time, but it's obvious that you've found something that we've missed. What is it?"

I swallowed my food and took a sip of coffee while considering his question. I knew I could give him the pat answer, but I wasn't sure he'd accept it. Simply to tell him that I'd found the living Lord might not register with him, either. Not really knowing what to say, I just opened my mouth and let the Jesus in me do the talking.

"Captain Porter, I found a source of living power. In addition to that, I found a bottomless well of love. The power can't be wielded without love, but the two of them together have completely changed my life. Where I was once rocked by anger and despair, I now have an assuring peace. Where I once served Satan, I now serve God."

"You talk as if God were a living person."

"He is," I replied. "He's alive in me, and through Him, I'm now the master of Satan."

"You talk as if Satan and hell exist."

"They do," I confirmed. "And if any man thinks he's his own master, then he's fooling himself." I turned and laid my hand on the Captain's arm. "God has given you a free choice as to which master you will serve, and you'll be rewarded accordingly, but service to yourself is no service at all. By default, you're serving the master of hell, because you're not serving God."

"Then what you're saying is this," the Captain reasoned. "Satan doesn't care whom you serve as long as it isn't God. In the end he'll be able to claim your soul, because you didn't choose to give it to the Lord."

"You've hit it right on the head," I agreed.

"I've never heard anyone talk about God the way you do, Mr. Ashcraft. How can you be certain that you're right?"

"Do you believe the Bible is the divine Word of God?"

"I suppose I do," he replied.

"Have you read His Word?"

The Captain remained silent for several minutes and then conceded, "Not really. When I've gone to church, I've heard the propers as they're read from scripture. This has generally been followed by a very learned and scholarly dissertation on their meaning, but I've never been excited by any of this."

"Then you've never really read the Bible for yourself."

"No, that hasn't been my thing," he admitted.

Reaching for a second sandwich, I posed another personal question for the Captain. "Exactly what is your thing?"

"I'm not quite sure." He paused for thought. "Perhaps it's doing what's best for me."

"With that goal in mind," I said, "let me answer your question about my being certain that I'm right. You see, Captain, I was wrong for so long that getting right with God became very important to me. I believe there's a God-shaped vacuum in every human heart, but too many of us spend our entire lives trying to fill it with the wrong thing. In a true sense, we find ourselves worshiping an object, or an accomplishment, more than God. We chase after wealth, or a new home, with the same zeal we should be using to seek the will of God. Do you understand what I'm saying?"

He sipped his coffee and nodded his head.

"You say that you believe in God," I continued, "yet you don't know Him. Is it possible that you may be giving some accomplishment more importance in your life, and because of it, you can't see beyond it?"

"It's possible," he conceded.

"Believing in God, as you say you do, have you ever considered asking Him to grant the accomplishment you're seeking?"

"Wouldn't that be rather selfish?" he asked.

"All things come from God," I flatly stated. "Everything you have is from Him. What makes you think that asking for what you want most would be selfish?"

"I've never thought of it that way," he answered.

"Don't misunderstand me, Captain. Just because you want something very badly doesn't necessarily mean that God wants you to have it. You have no way of knowing what the gaining of your accomplishment might do to you, but God does. It's possible that what you desire may be the worst thing in the world for you, or even better yet, God may use your desire to give you a gift of greater value. He might even give you the power to accomplish miracles!"

Taking a bite of my sandwich, I watched Captain Porter assimilate what I'd just said. A deep frown creased his forehead as he spoke.

"Does God actually give men such power?"

"I believe He does," I answered. "When we want it for His glory and not our own." The Captain was on the hook and I started reeling him in. "The secret is to make God's glory become your glory. You have to make His will your will. You have to become one with Him. You have to invite Him into your heart and make Him the Lord of your life." I smiled at him and added, "Once you've done this, the Bible becomes the most exciting book in the world and its meaning is made clear to you."

"Then I want it!" the Captain emphatically stated. "How do I get it?"

"It's simple," I said, "you surrender yourself, your sins and your life to God and then ask for the baptism of the Holy Spirit." I explained how John had baptized Jesus in water and foretold of the spiritual baptism that was still to come. I read the scriptures that told how Jesus had commanded His disciples to wait for the Day of Pentecost and what happened to them. When I closed my Bible in my lap, Captain Porter was ready. We prayed together in the name of Jesus, and He honored our prayers.

I watched the love of God fill the vacuum in the Captain's heart, and I heard him speak to God with the assurance that he was being understood. The living Lord had entered another human soul, and I felt the Holy Spirit around us. When Captain Porter walked back to the flight deck, I knew that Jesus was now flying the aircraft.

Snapping off my reading lamp, I leaned back in my seat and mentally returned to the Houston of Elizabeth, David, Carol and me.

# Chapter 12
# MORE THAN A MAN CAN STAND

*"And the peace of God, which passeth all understanding,
shall keep your hearts and minds through Christ Jesus. "*
**Philippians 4:7**

At the time of Carole's illness, my ministry in the Full Gospel
Business Men's Fellowship had grown. I was one of the
organization's International Directors. I sent out healing prayer
requests, for Carole and Elizabeth, to chapters all over the
world. Carole felt the power of those prayers and recovered
from her exploratory operation. Her color returned, and she
regained enough strength to be discharged from St. Luke's, but
Elizabeth didn't respond at all.

My wife continued to lose weight, and her lovely face was
becoming deeply creased with lines of worry, concern and self-
condemnation. Even with Carole back home and at work,
Elizabeth went further downhill. It was almost as if she were
blaming herself for Carole's affliction. She was blindly searching
within herself for some sin, or lack of faith, that might cause
God to punish her through Carole.

I was desperate to find some solution to all these problems,
and about that time I began receiving phone calls and letters
from men and women all over the country. Many of them were
ministers, but they all said the same thing. "I've received a word
from the Lord," they would say, "and He's commanded me to
come to Houston and pray for your wife and daughter." In
almost every case, they would add, "But I haven't the money to

travel, and I do have to make a living."

My vulnerability was open to this. I paid their expenses and gave them generous honorariums for their prayers. In a sense, I was trying to buy God's blessing for two of the women I loved. I know the prayers did not hurt, and I blame no one for my susceptibility, but I cannot truthfully say those prayers produced any fruit.

With Carole seemingly back on her feet, and Shirley nearby to watch over her mother, I felt I could do more good serving the Lord in my ministry than by staying home and brooding. I began traveling and giving witness again. On short trips, Carole would come with me. Every time she stood and sang for the Full Gospel Business Men, I would remember the happier times.

I would think of days when she glowed with joy. Like the day she returned from Washington, D.C., after visiting the White House and singing for President and Mrs. Johnson. Her vivacious spirit just bubbled when she told me, "Daddy, they took me everywhere in the presidential limousine. They even offered me a job if I wanted to come to Washington."

I would watch the warmth of her love spread over everyone and say to myself, "Lord, You can't take Carole away from us. She's just beginning her ministry for Your glory. We all see You in her and rejoice. You've given her an angel's voice and we praise You for it. Let her stay with us a while longer."

Six months after her release from St. Luke's, Carole had a relapse. Once again, I was driven to my knees. Elizabeth's helpless and exhausted tears formed a grieving harmony with my prayers. After treatment, our daughter came home a second time, and we realized she'd never been healed. The doctors tried to give us hope, but their eyes betrayed them. We all knew Carole was dying.

Tommy Jr., Shirley, David, Elizabeth and I couldn't help

ourselves. Every minute each of us spent with Carole was selfishly cherished. I know we projected our sadness to her, and in a way, I think it helped prepare her for what was ahead. She loved the Lord with all her heart, soul and mind, and I know He loved her. Jesus was gentle with us all. He gave us four more months of her happy spirit. She seemed more concerned over her loss of hair, because of the treatments, than she did with dying. Her other great concern was the deteriorating health of her mother. They would spend hours together, with Carole trying to lift Elizabeth from the morass of her depression.

With my daughter dying and my wife isolating herself in mental anguish, Satan hit me with another burden. Out of a work force of more than 130 people, 19 union members at the bakery went on strike. Frank and I tried every means at our disposal to meet their demands, but the economics of reality prevented it. Our customers began finding other sources of supply. We tried to maintain production, but failed. Those workers who would come in were punished by having their automobile tires slashed. We had to add the expense of special police protection to our already overextended resources.

When Carole had her second relapse and returned to the hospital, I was near the very end of my financial resources. I knew that God would have to tell me what to do, because I was out of ideas. In my desperation I even tried to call God on the phone.

Elizabeth and I were living at the hospital, and when I simply couldn't stand watching Carole fade away, I would search out a phone booth and call God. I'd put in my coin, get a dial tone and dial three numbers: one for the Father, one for the Son, and one for the Holy Ghost. I'd speak into that silent phone and wait for an answer.

"Lord, I don't know what I'm going to do. Sometimes I feel

like I'm going to die, but I can't. I'm going broke, Carole's fixin'
to come to You, Elizabeth's sick and the bakery's strikebound.
How much longer must I bear all this?"

I believe in talking to the Lord like that. I think we can lay it
on the line with Him. He knows everything, anyway, and
sometimes I think He wants to know if we're aware of
everything around us.

"Lord," I'd say, "all this has been building up and going on for
over a year and a half. When's it going to stop?"

After doing this several times, I decided to change the
approach of my conversations with God. I was at the end of my
rope and something had to be done.

"Father, You know what my problems are. Please give me
some of the solutions. Let me work them out so that we can get
on with Your business here on earth."

In this phone prayer, I wasn't whining and crying for mercy. I
was asking for guidance and direction. I was submitting myself
to the will of God. When we do this, the action that follows can
be both joyful and sad, but at least it isn't more of the same.

Going directly to the bakery from the hospital one morning
in October, 1970, I was greeted by four pickets. One of them
was a foreman who'd been with us from the very start. Seeing
him with a sign on his shoulder quickened my heart, and I knew
I had to trust the Lord for guidance. I still had my keys in my
hand when I got out of the car. Jesus gave me the words that I
spoke.

"Sam," I said, holding up my keys, "we've been forced to the
end. I'm going to lock her up today, and when I do, she's going
to stay locked. Frank and I can get along without the bakery,
but I don't think you can. You've had a good steady job here,
but once this key turns, that job will no longer exist!"

He looked at the other three pickets before he responded.

"Mr. Ashcraft, don't do it. This doesn't have to be the end." His eyes found the other faces, and, pleading more with them than with me, he added, "You've been too good to us for that. You lent me the money to buy my house." Pointing to another picket, he continued, "And you paid for Pat's new baby. Half the cars in the company parking lot were purchased with your help." Throwing down his sign, he proclaimed, "I'm comin' back to work!" Three more signs were added to his, and we all went inside.

The strike was broken, but our customers were gone. We got back into operation, but we couldn't regain our market. Here again, I had to turn to God for the answer. He's such an excellent Businessman that I can't understand why anyone ever feels that God shouldn't be part of the business world.

Carole had recovered enough to leave St. Luke's, and Elizabeth and I were at home. My wife hadn't shown any improvement, but it seemed as if our lives were getting back under control. I was sitting alone in our living room when I felt an urgent need for God.

"Lord, we've got a problem," I prayed. "Our trucks are returning to the bakery every day with more stale products on them than we're selling. You've solved our strike, but this may be worse. What should we do?"

He answered me with the most brilliantly simple solution. "Tom," He said, "quit baking all that fancy stuff that you're bringing back! Quit trying to service the customers that demand it! Go after the institutional business! Cater to the hotels, restaurants, hospitals, schools, jails and other places that use bread as part of their service."

I got out of that chair and called Frank. I was so excited I could hardly talk. Frank got excited. God had given us the answer. By restricting the type of products we produced, we could bake less, and because our returned products would be greatly reduced, we'd earn more.

Following God's orders, the Ashcraft Baking Company began to prosper again. Elizabeth was beginning to hold her own, and I could see a tiny light at the end of the tunnel of our troubles. It looked as if everything was coming up roses when Carole went under again. Her third reprieve had lasted only two months.

It was March, 1971, when Carole submitted to open heart surgery. We prayed that our doctors could cut that growth away and purge her weakened body of its poison. She approached this with total confidence in God. She said, "Daddy, I didn't get healed, but maybe the Lord wants my doctors to do that as a witness to them." Her smile gave me strength when she observed, "Maybe I can help them find something that will help others and if this is what God wants, then so be it."

This time I stayed in the hospital with her. With her suffering, the days seemed endless, but she and I did find a new joy. During the times that she was awake, we would visit with a quiet closeness that we'd never shared before. We would talk about the things she did when she was small. Her entire lifetime, short as it was, seemed to have been a living witness of love and joy. She would softly sing the songs I loved, and her tender heart would take wings on the melody. We know that Jesus shared those private moments with us, because I could see Him in her big, beautiful, dark eyes. She and I shared our silent tears with the poignant love that grew between us. One evening, David brought Elizabeth to the hospital with him, and I heard her speak a lie that was straight from Satan.

Calling me out of the room to a secluded corner in the hallway, she stood on tiptoe and whispered in my ear. "Daddy, God has told me that if I'll give my life to the lepers, He'll save

Carole. I've called some people in Arkansas, but they won't accept me because I'm not a trained nurse. But the people in Africa want me if you'll pay my expenses." A note of pleading entered her voice. "Please, Daddy, will you pay my way?"

This wasn't from God, and I tried to reason her out of it, but she insisted. In the end, I had to flatly refuse, and the look in my wife's eyes will stay with me forever. Following this, I started back to the phone booth.

I wouldn't allow myself to cry in front of Carole. I saved that for my moments alone with the phone. When I'd come back to the room, she'd take one look at me and say, "Daddy, you've been crying; please don't."

One evening toward the end of March, I was speaking in the phone mouthpiece, when an almost audible thought formed in my mind. "Tommy, I'm going to take her in five days." I knew it wasn't God.

I screamed back, "No, Satan, you can't take her, and even if you do, God will raise her from the dead!"

"No, Tommy, I'm taking her in five days."

I was positive it wasn't God. My birthday was just five days away, and God wouldn't give me Carole's death as a present. He couldn't possibly intend such a thing. Each evening, when I'd go back to the phone, the message was repeated, minus one day. On the evening of the fourth day, Carole was very weak. I ordered a special nurse for her and gave instructions that I was to be awakened if anything happened.

My bed was right beside Carole's. They'd given her special care that day because her arms were so swollen from the shots she'd been taking. Most of her hair was gone, and they hadn't allowed her a mirror for some time. Because of her condition, we didn't talk that night. With the nurse's assurance that I'd be wakened, I finally drifted into an uneasy sleep.

The nurse shook me in the night and whispered, "Come quickly, Mr. Ashcraft, Carole has gone."

I rolled out of my bed, still half-asleep. Seeing the oxygen mask off Carole's face, I quickly replaced it.

"No, Mr. Ashcraft," the nurse said, "Carole's gone! That won't do any good."

"What time is it?" I demanded.

"12:31, Wednesday morning," she said.

It was the fifth day! It was my birthday, and Carole was gone! She'd been taken! She'd been stolen from me! If it wasn't Satan, then God was a thief!

They got me out of the room and sent for the chaplain. On the outside, I must have appeared calm, because when the young man approached me, he asked, "Can I help you?"

"Have you ever lost a daughter?" I asked.

"No, I'm not married."

"Then how can you help me? You can't even understand."

God, in His grace, then poured a blessing on me. The realization that He was supreme settled over me. A new understanding swept through me. How can anyone help someone when he's never experienced the pain himself? How can you help a person when he's gone broke, when you've never been broke yourself? How can you help someone who has lost a daughter, when you've never lost a daughter yourself? How can you help a man find God, when you haven't found Him yourself?

All of this flooded over me, but the pain of my loss remained. Jesus said He suffered all things, and that's why He understands. Was I going to have to suffer all things? My pain increased! I had to be alone! God had robbed me! Carole was gone! My tears of grief finally began to flow, but I had to force them back. I still had to go home and tell Elizabeth. I feared what the news would do to her, but she had to be told.

Standing outside her bedroom door, I had to steel myself against what I expected. I'd told her she couldn't go to Africa and minister to the lepers. Would she blame herself and me for Carole's death? Would she consider that I'd stopped her from obeying God? I knew God didn't strike such bargains, but would she understand? She was ill. Would this terrible news press her further into her sickness? In my mind, God was a thief, and I didn't feel free to pray to a thief. I turned the knob and opened the door. Elizabeth was standing just inside. She may have been standing there for hours, just waiting. I started to speak, but her raised hand stopped me.

"Don't tell me. I already know. Carole's passed away. I knew it last night. I knew it at midnight."

Elizabeth may have been crying, but all her tears were gone. She was facing reality for the first time in 22 months. Her recovery had begun. My pain was increasing, and the anguish in my heart was almost beyond bearing. A serene smile filled my wife's face, and she said, "Daddy, everything's going to be all right."

Everything wasn't all right! Carole was gone! Turning away, I went into the living room to be alone. "Why did You take her, Lord?" I asked. "Why did You steal her?"

The voice in my heart spoke with a gentle softness. "I didn't steal her, Tommy. She has always been Mine. You gave her to Me. Don't you remember?"

It was true. I had given her to God. She was His, but I still didn't understand. "God," I said, "why?"

"Heaven isn't made up of just old people. Everything is in perfect balance here. We have babies, small children, young adults, men and women and oldsters. Tommy, you own the bakery, and if you want to drive one of the trucks home at night, you can. You own them. You're not stealing one when you drive it home. What makes you think I had to steal Carole? She's here with Me, and that's all you need to know."

I'd been given my answer. It was the only answer that made any sense. I think Elizabeth got the same answer and understood it. She and I were once again in union with God. Carole had helped Him give us this priceless gift and we could rejoice in her victory.

In the months that followed Carole's death, the bakery continued to grow. We were producing one-third less product, but realizing our greatest profits. After two years of this activity, I took a lesson from Bill Carroll's book and went to Frank.

"Little brother," I said, "I want to go fulltime for the Lord. Can you buy my half of the bakery?"

We came to an agreement and I signed it over to him. My Full Gospel Business Men's ministry was growing and demanding more of my time. A man was needed to travel all over the world to assist in forming new chapters. That duty fell to me. Starting in 1973, I entered the ministry, as a layman, on a fulltime basis. In a true sense, I started an exciting safari for God. It has taken me to all corners of the earth, often with Elizabeth beside me. We have shared the danger and thrill of bringing people to the Lord. Someday, I'll ask Jesus if I can tell that story, but for now, it isn't finished.

I must have fallen asleep, because the landing announcement for Houston International Airport awoke me. Looking out the window, I caught the reflection of the man beside me. He smiled and touched my shoulder. "You've done well, Tommy," the voice in my heart said, "but there's still a great deal to accomplish. Elizabeth will be waiting for you on the ground, and your next assignment will come to you in a few days. I'm always with you, Tommy, remember that."

   I turned to see the face of Him, but He was once again inside me, and I could only feel His all-encompassing love.

# EPILOGUE

*"He that hath an ear, let him hear what the Spirit saith unto the churches."*

**Revelation 2:29**

When the apostle Paul wrote to Timothy, he said, "Let the elders that rule well be counted worthy of double honor, especially they who labor in the word and doctrine." Tommy is just such an elder. He is a man, and as such is weak, but he loves the Lord our God with all his heart, soul and mind. In writing Tommy's story, I found the Lord Jesus ministering to us both. With the power of the Holy Spirit, Tom and I became one. We were bound together with holy cords of love and allowed to share an intimacy with God that comes to few men.

I felt Tommy's hurt, anger and pride as if they were mine. I re-experienced the pull of alcohol which we both have shared. His lust reflected my own. We were brothers in sin and now we cherish our brotherhood in God. I am my brother's keeper and when he hurts, I hurt. When he weeps, I weep. When he laughs, I laugh. His joy is my joy and his peace is my peace.

Tommy is an International Vice President of the Full Gospel Business Men's Fellowship International. He's charged with the ministry of forming new chapters all over the world. With the help and power of the Holy Spirit, he's fulfilling that charge. His dear wife Elizabeth is truly a Spirit-filled helpmate. Together they reflect the glory of God in His kingdom here on earth. We chose to stop this story at a point of beginning, because their "safari with God" is still going on. At some point in the future, when Jesus allows us, we may write that story.

But for now, let us pray as Jesus has taught us. "Our Father which art in heaven, hallowed be thy name. Thy kingdom come. Thy will be done on earth, as it is in heaven. Give us this day our daily bread. And forgive us our debts, as we forgive our debtors. And lead us not into temptation, but deliver us from evil: For thine is the kingdom, and the power, and the glory, forever. Amen."

**En agape,**
**Max Call**
**Garland, Texas**